Date: 1/1/20

**332.6 KOE
Koesterich, Russ,
Portfolio construction for
today's markets :**

Portfolio Construction for Today's Markets

Portfolio Construction for Today's Markets

A practitioner's guide to the essentials of asset allocation

Russ Koesterich

Hh

Hh Harriman House

HARRIMAN HOUSE LTD
18 College Street
Petersfield
Hampshire
GU31 4AD
GREAT BRITAIN
Tel: +44 (0)1730 233870
Email: enquiries@harriman-house.com
Website: www.harriman-house.com

First published in Great Britain in 2018
Copyright © Russ Koesterich

The right of Russ Koesterich to be identified as the Author has been asserted in accordance with the Copyright, Design and Patents Act 1988.

Hardback ISBN: 978-0-85719-629-3
eBook ISBN: 978-0-85719-630-9

British Library Cataloguing in Publication Data
A CIP catalogue record for this book can be obtained from the British Library.

Whilst every effort has been made to ensure that information in this book is accurate, no liability can be accepted for any loss incurred in any way whatsoever by any person relying solely on the information contained herein.

No responsibility for loss occasioned to any person or corporate body acting or refraining to act as a result of reading material in this book can be accepted by the Publisher, by the Author, or by the employers of the Author.

To Alice and Palmer.
Thank you for your unfailing support, encouragement and for putting up with long absences and too many interrupted vacations.

Every owner of a physical copy of this edition of

Portfolio Construction for Today's Markets

can download the eBook for free direct from us at Harriman House, in a format that can be read on any eReader, tablet or smartphone.

Simply head to:

ebooks.harriman-house.com/portfoliotoday

to get your free eBook now.

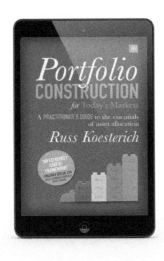

Contents

About the author

Mr Koesterich is a financial services veteran with 22 years' experience in the industry. Since 2005 he has worked at Barclays Global Investors and BlackRock, the world's largest asset manager, with over $6 trillion in assets.

Mr Koesterich is currently a Portfolio Manager of the BlackRock Global Allocation Funds. In that capacity Mr Koesterich is responsible for driving asset allocation and risk management for BlackRock's largest investment team, managing approximately $80 billion. Prior to his current role Mr Koesterich served as the Global Chief Investment Strategist for BlackRock as well as the Chief Investment Strategist for the iShares business, the world's largest provider of exchange traded funds (ETFs). Prior to joining BlackRock (then BGI) in 2005, Mr Koesterich was the Chief North American Strategist for State Street Global Markets in Boston.

Mr Koesterich is a frequent contributor to the financial news, including CNBC, Bloomberg, and Fox Business television, the *Wall Street Journal*, *Financial Times* and MarketWatch. He is the author of two previous books.

Mr Koesterich holds a BA from Brandeis University, a JD from Boston College Law School and an MBA from Columbia Business School. He is also a Chartered Financial Analyst (CFA).

Preface

What this book covers and who this book is for

Since coming out of the financial crisis in 2009, investors have had both the best of times and the worst of times. Stock markets have soared, helping create significant wealth for those who have stayed invested. Others have struggled, sitting in cash awaiting a return to a more normal rate environment.

The financial advisor is caught in the middle. Some clients are perpetually enraged that their multi-asset class portfolio is not keeping up with hot tech stocks. Many older or more conservative clients are facing a completely different challenge: low, and sometimes negative, interest rates defy both logic and experience. For the latter group, many keep searching for that now almost mythical *5% yield*, a level that many investors view as a virtual birthright.

This book will hopefully offer a solution for both sets of clients – those shooting for the moon and those just looking to fund their retirement.

My approach is to tackle the challenge of asset allocation through the lens of portfolio construction. What's the difference? To my mind portfolio construction is to asset allocation what engineering is to physics: the practical application used to build actual things. In this case, what we're looking to build are portfolios geared towards achieving client goals.

That is a tall order in itself. It is also a long-term goal. As such, there is little here to tell an investor whether emerging market stocks or silver futures will outperform next year. I've also intentionally avoided questions regarding implementation. Many investors are still struggling to decide whether to focus on actively managed mutual funds or exchange traded funds (ETFs) that simply try to mimic an index. The short answer is, you can use both. While the choice is not trivial, the first and to my mind more important question is: can you build a robust asset allocation?

Given that goal, the reader can approach this book in two ways. First, I've provided a relatively simple, step-by-step approach to portfolio construction. A second group will come to this book with their own predispositions and methods. That is fine as well. There are many ways to forecast returns, estimate risk and put the pieces together. For this second group I would still recommend the book, but less as a manual and more as a manifesto. Even for those who feel comfortable with their own methods, hopefully the book can serve as a reinforcement of a few key principles: the primacy of risk, the need for explicit investment goals and a healthy appreciation of why it is difficult to forecast returns.

In the end, both the advisor and end client are left with the unavoidable reality that excess return requires risk. That said, hopefully the book will provide some insight on how to minimize and manage that risk. A properly constructed portfolio should lead to fewer panicked, late-night phone calls. More importantly, it will help prevent clients from abandoning long-term plans. To the extent a better designed portfolio will help mitigate the biggest risk – the risk of giving up and hiding under the mattress – both the client and advisor benefit.

How this book is structured

I have arranged the book as seven chapters that trace the different areas someone constructing a portfolio in today's investment climate needs to consider. These are as follows.

Chapter 1 covers setting investment goals. The next two chapters cover the implementation of those goals, with Chapter 2 devoted to constraints and Chapter 3 focused on measuring risk.

In Chapter 4, I cover the arguments for diversification. Chapter 5 offers a different perspective, introducing factor investing as a different prism through which to view your portfolio. Chapter 6 covers the various methods for forecasting returns, a key input to any portfolio construction process.

Finally, in Chapter 7 I bring everything together and cover the subject of how to build a portfolio while bearing in mind all that has gone before in the previous six chapters.

Introduction

The art of asset allocation

Most investors are drawn to stock picking. Uncovering a little known value stock or finding the next big growth company is the fun part of the job. For those with the requisite skill, successful stock picking can also help boost returns. In a few, rare instances it will make you and your clients rich.

Unfortunately, few possess the stock picking prescience of Warren Buffett. The hard truth is most investors struggle to beat the market through stock selection. In addition, an exclusive focus on finding a winning stock, or for that matter a winning mutual fund, ignores the bigger challenge.

No investor should ever live or die based on a single stock or investment idea. It is the *mix* of stocks, bonds, cash and other investments that drives long-term performance. Asset allocation, stock picking's less glamorous cousin, is where investment goals are achieved or missed.

Asset allocation is the art of combining different investment assets to build a portfolio aligned with the investor's objectives and respectful of their limitations. More than picking the right stock or owning a particular bond, it is the allocation to these assets that drives returns.

Yet, despite the importance of asset allocation, there is little agreement on how to do it most effectively.

The primacy of risk

Many investors have a tendency to start building portfolios with a view on the markets. While understandable, this skips a few, critical steps. There can be no asset allocation until you define the return you are trying to generate, the risk you are willing to tolerate and the constraints you need to impose.

The challenge, as seasoned investors have come to realize, is that most people either don't know their risk tolerance, or tend to grossly overestimate it. At least, they overestimate until things turn bad. This results in a lot of unnecessary pain.

Not only is a less volatile portfolio conducive to a good night's sleep, but more importantly it is a necessary prerequisite to sticking to an investment plan. If the volatility of an investor's portfolio is outside his or her comfort zone, they are more likely to sell, probably at exactly the wrong time.

A related challenge is getting investors to define their constraints, ideally in a sensible fashion. Constraints can be thought of as financial no-fly zones. Some investors, to their detriment, won't invest outside of their home country. Others avoid certain asset classes, such as commodities. Most of these constraints come with a cost. In an effort to avoid risk, many investors wind up with a portfolio that is actually riskier than it needs to be.

A dearth of income

Defining investor objectives and teasing out their constraints has never been easy. More recently investors have been contending with a new problem, one more directly tied to markets and the economy. Thanks to a sluggish recovery following the 2007–09 financial crisis, coupled with the creativity of central bankers, interest rates remain stuck near historic lows. Bonds, the traditional source of income, pay a fraction of what they did 20 or 30 years ago.

This is not an easy problem to fix. If the part a portfolio allocated to bonds is producing little to no return, there are only two choices: buy riskier assets or dramatically lower investment return expectations.

The net result is that the old rules of asset allocation do not apply any more. Placing your clients' assets in a 60/40 stocks/bonds portfolio and leaving the market to do the rest is unlikely to work as well over the next few decades as it has in recent years. A refresh is needed.

Rethinking the model

This book is intended to provide some of the answers. Humans do many things well, but managing money is generally not one of them. Fear and greed get in the way, no matter how smart we may be. Managing the emotional side of investments is every bit, and arguably more, important than the analytical side. It therefore helps to have a plan.

In an effort to produce that plan, this book breaks down the asset allocation process. The aim is to turn portfolio construction into a series of steps that demystify the exercise. Starting with setting objectives, the book covers all parts of the process, including the importance of risk, generating return assumptions, and combining assets in a risk-controlled manner.

Recognizing that *combining assets in a risk-controlled manner* is not nearly as exciting as *how to retire rich at 40*, some may have already lost interest. For anyone with the more modest goal of building robust portfolios to meet client goals, please keep reading.

1

Money for Nothing: The Challenges of a Low-Rate World

"THIS", "TIME", "IT'S" and "different" have been said to be the four most dangerous words in finance. In the past they've very often preceded an argument attempting to justify a dicey investment scheme, overvalued asset or sometimes outright fraud. With that disclaimer in hand, in one big, important respect investors are today facing a very profound "this time it's different" moment.

Money managers have been following the mantra of *long-term portfolios* for decades now. Success may have varied depending upon the period and how well the investor stuck to their plan, but for the most part, the classic approaches worked. Simple asset allocation models were effective.

The most well-known asset allocation model was based on a simple formula: invest 60% in stocks and 40% in bonds. This simple formula – the 60/40 model – provided a reasonable balance between long-term growth, income and manageable volatility. In certain decades, notably the 1980s and 1990s, when both stocks and bond markets rallied in unison, the 60/40 model provided better returns than most had expected.

If 60/40 has worked so well in the past, why change now? The simple but uncomfortable answer is: "this time it's different."

One potential argument for why things are different this time is valuations. As of this writing, stock markets are in the ninth year of a bull market and equity valuations, particularly in the United States, are stretched. While this does not necessarily suggest stock prices are in danger of an imminent collapse, it does suggest lower returns on equities going forward. That said, these high valuations are not really a game changer. After all, stocks have been overvalued in the past, before then dropping in price, and then subsequently bouncing back.

It is also worth noting that while obvious in hindsight, bear markets are rarely obvious before the fact. Even for those lucky enough to get out in time, few are so skilled as to re-enter the market at the exact bottom. More often they miss most of the subsequent rally before re-entering the market. The prospect or even likelihood of a bear market – we know at some point in the future one will occur – is not sufficient to throw out well-established asset allocation rules.

If a creaky stock market is not the game changer, what is? In one word: bonds.

It's bonds

It is a cornerstone of finance that there is a time value to money. People prefer their money today rather than a year from now. Accordingly, for me to lend you my money you need to pay me a rate of interest. While interest rates have fluctuated dramatically over the thousands of years humans have been lending to each other, they have almost always been comfortably above zero. That can no longer be taken for granted.

The big change that has occurred in recent years, the one that upends the whole process of building a long-term portfolio, is what has happened to interest rates. They have plunged.

This brings us to bonds. While traditionally thought of as the boring, less sexy cousin of stocks, bonds are critical to a portfolio. They play three important roles: income, stability and a hedge against equity market volatility (in other words, diversification). However, all three roles are now under threat.

Income

The most obvious change has been income, or more accurately the lack of it. Today most bonds pay practically no income, even before accounting for taxes and inflation, because yields are so low. This means that under a 60% stocks, 40% bonds arrangement, a good chunk of the portfolio is doing little to produce returns. As a result, the rest of the portfolio – the part not invested in bonds – has to contribute more to make up the shortfall.

The income challenge is further exacerbated by the fact that a prolonged period of low rates has pushed up the valuation on other types of assets that generate income. In the United States in 2017, many dividend-paying stocks trade near record valuations as investors flee the bond market in search of a reasonable yield. As bond investors migrate to dividend-paying stocks in search of income, prices have risen. Higher prices mean that the dividend yield – defined as the annual dividend divided by the price – on many of these stocks and sectors is significantly lower than in the past.

As an example, consider the utilities sector. Utility companies, which are typically valued for their high dividends, now offer a yield of closer to 2%–3% rather than 4%–5%. This suggests that even if an income-oriented investor is willing to accept the greater risk of owning a stock rather than a bond, many of those stocks are now providing a significantly lower dividend yield than was the case 20 years ago.

Stability

Low interest rates inject another complication into the mix. A side effect of low rates is that bond durations, i.e. the sensitivity of the bond to changes in rates, are elevated relative to historical norms. Higher durations translate into more interest rate risk. In more visceral terms, as duration rises, bondholders will experience greater losses when and if interest rates rise. So, as things stand today, even a small rise in rates will inflict significant losses on the bond portion of portfolios.

Diversification

Low rates and higher durations imply less income and more risk. However, up until recently investors could at least rely on bonds for the third characteristic: diversification.

Even though rates have been low, bonds have still done one thing reliably well. For most of the post-crisis period they have provided a hedge against equity risk. In other words, when stocks have gone down, bonds have typically gone up. In more quantitative terms, bonds have had a consistent negative correlation with stocks.

Negative correlation is the holy grail in building portfolios. The negative correlation between stocks and bonds has helped to cushion the blow when markets have been volatile. In the few recent instances when stocks have declined sharply – summer of 2011 or early 2016 – bonds have been there to help mitigate the damage. Going forward, if stock/bond correlations are not as consistently negative, bonds will be less effective in mitigating overall portfolio risk.

Thus, we have established that the three priority roles for bonds in a portfolio – income, stability and diversification – are challenged by the current environment. We will return to look at these three areas in more detail later in the chapter.

Low for long, very long

Before taking each of these three challenges in turn, it is worth exploring why rates are as low as they are. Equally important is how low rates are relative to historical norms.

To say that interest rates remain close to historic lows sounds a bit like hyperbole. At least in the United States, the Federal Reserve has begun the process of tightening monetary conditions by raising short-term interest rates. This process is likely to continue in the coming years, which should see short-term rates continue to rise above the 0% level that defined much of the post-crisis environment.

At the same time, long-term bond yields have also risen. US ten-year government bond yields are roughly 1% higher than they were at the lows during the summer of 2016. Is it really accurate to still talk about ultra-low rates?

Despite marginally tighter monetary policy in the United States and a modest increase in bond yields, by any historical measure interest rates remain close to levels that would have been deemed unlikely, if not impossible, ten years ago. A good example of how truly unusual this period is comes from the United Kingdom, where financial records extend further back in time.

One of the longest continuous series of interest rates is from the Bank of England (BOE). Founded in 1694, the Bank of England has been setting short-term interest rates for the United Kingdom even before there was a United Kingdom (the Act of Union with Scotland occurred 13 years later).

According to the Bank of England's website, the bank's official rate was 6% in 1694. To be fair, there are periods when it dropped well below that level. The policy rate fell as low as 2% during the mid- and late 19th century.

However, during the bank's +300 year history, short-term rates never fell below 1% until early in 2009, when it lowered the rate to 0.50% (see Chart 1.1). The rate reached a new low, 0.25%, in the summer of 2016 following the UK referendum to leave the European Union. When referencing ultra-low rates, the BOE's policy rate provides an excellent example of just how unusual the current environment is. Going back over 300 years, interest rates have truly never been lower.

Chart 1.1: UK Bank of England official base rate (%)

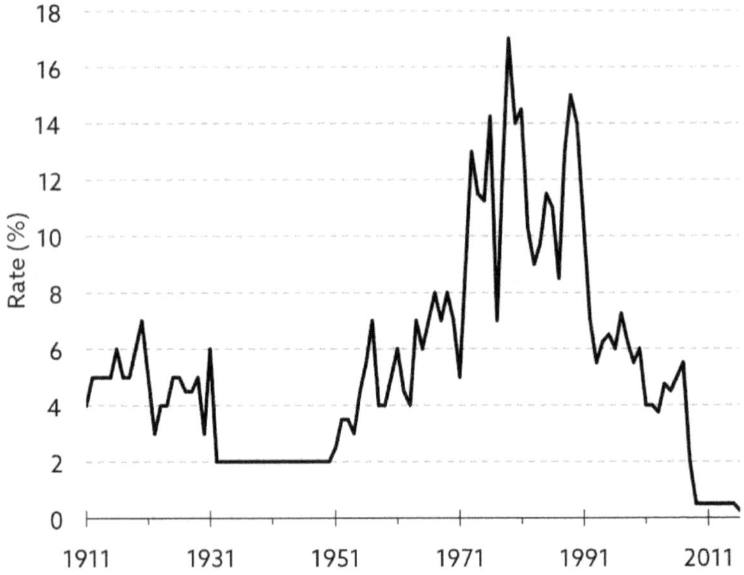

Source: Bloomberg, March 2017.

US monetary policy does not extend back into the 17th century, but the pattern is the same. The Federal Reserve lowered US short-term rates to effectively zero shortly after the 2007–09 financial crisis. While the Fed has subsequently lifted rates several times, at the time of writing the federal funds rate, the rate that sets the cost of overnight borrowing for banks, remains at around 1%.

These historically low rates are even more astounding when you consider that by 2017 it had been nearly a decade since the financial crisis. Many will recall that the period of ultra-low interest rates was supposed to be a temporary step, taken in extremis to prevent another Great Depression. At the time, few imagined near-zero short-term rates as a permanent fixture of financial markets.

Today's environment of near zero short-term rates and paltry long-term rates is a far cry from what most investors, particularly older ones, had become accustomed to. Any investor in their mid-to-late 50s started out in a very different world.

In the early 1980s the Fed, along with many of the world's other central banks, was in the midst of a fight against stubbornly high inflation. Inflation has been a problem for many countries since the 1960s. The typical response by central banks was to raise short-term interest rates. Higher short-term rates, coupled with justifiable inflation fears, pushed up long-term rates to levels that seem impossibly high today. To emphasize just how different the rate environment was, the federal funds rate reached a peak of nearly 20% in the early 1980s!

Nor was it the case that higher rates went out of fashion with disco. Even in the 1990s, a period of generally tame inflation, the federal funds rate still averaged around 5% (see Chart 1.2). Today's norm of near-zero short-term rates has no precedent, at least not within living memory.

Chart 1.2: US federal funds rate (%)

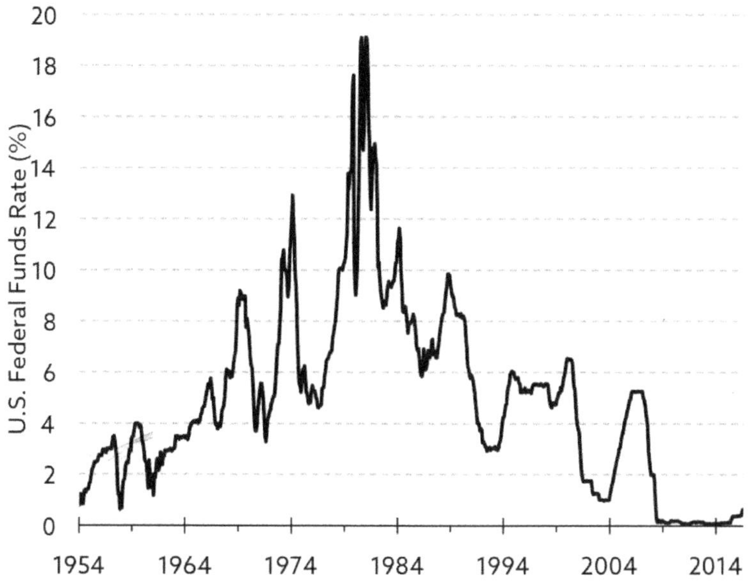

Source: Bloomberg, March 2017.

Less than zero

Alone, low short-term rates may not be such a big deal. After all, there is always the additional option of longer-term bonds. Even if short-term rates are low, historically investors have received higher yields in longer-dated bonds.

Also, in the past long-term rates have been set by the market, not by central banks. Surely this segment of the market has behaved more rationally?

As most are painfully aware, the situation for long-term bonds is little better. While it is possible to find higher yields for longer-dated bonds, in some instances the situation is even more surreal. While rates are higher the longer you go out on the yield curve, it is not clear they are anywhere close to sufficiently high to justify the incremental risk of a bond with a 10, 20 or 30 year maturity.

Long-term bonds by their nature carry more risk in the form of higher durations or rate sensitivity. The risk of buying long-dated bonds is that if rates go up, the bond price goes down more than it would for a shorter-dated bond. Traditionally, investors have been compensated for that risk with a rate 200–300 basis points above the prevailing rate on short-term debt. Today, that premium has become far less reliable.

As it turns out, in a slow-growth world of near-zero short-term rates, financial institutions are willing to lend money for prolonged periods for very little return. Not only are there long-term bonds yielding close to zero, there is an even more arresting phenomenon: negative long-term interest rates.

Those who buy bonds at a negative interest rate are guaranteed to lose money in nominal terms if they hold to maturity. At one point in 2016, more than $10 trillion in global bonds was trading with a negative interest rate (see Chart 1.3). Nor was this strange state of affairs limited to government bonds. At one point, corporate bonds also started trading with a negative yield as well.

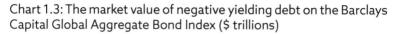

Chart 1.3: The market value of negative yielding debt on the Barclays Capital Global Aggregate Bond Index ($ trillions)

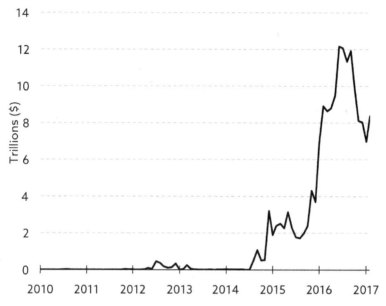

Source: Bloomberg, March 2017.

Thus far, negative yields have primarily been confined to continental Europe and Japan, where growth and inflation have been exceptionally low and central banks have pushed short-term policy rates into negative territory. The situation in the United States and United Kingdom never got quite so silly.

Still, greater sobriety only went so far. US ten-year Treasury yields did hit an all-time low of 1.36% in July of 2016 while ten-year UK Gilts yields bottomed several months later at approximately 0.50%. While bond yields have subsequently bounced in both countries, even today, nearly a decade after the financial crisis, long-term rates remain a fraction of their long-term average.

The global economy: older, slower and less productive

All of this raises the obvious question: have absurdly low rates simply been a bout of investor insanity, i.e. a bond market bubble, or is there a more rational explanation? And perhaps more interesting for those thinking about their asset allocation over the next one to two decades: can this period of ultra-low interest rates continue much longer?

In answering both questions it is useful to consider what economic and other factors drive interest rates. There are a number of theories to explain interest rates, most beyond the scope of this book. Suffice to say that interest rates do not occur in a vacuum. While predicting rates is no easier than forecasting stock prices, there are factors that can help explain the level of rates.

Deceleration in nominal GDP

Interest rates are the price of money and as with all market prices, they typically reflect both supply and demand. The demand side of the equation comes from the real economy. Faster economic growth equates to stronger demand for credit, i.e. money. Over the long term, interest rates generally move in-line with nominal GDP (NGDP), the sum of both real growth plus inflation. During the past 50 years, US nominal GDP has explained approximately 35% of the variation in ten-year Treasury yields (see Chart 1.4).

While not the full story, the multi-decade deceleration in nominal GDP, itself a function of a slowdown in real growth and inflation, explains a good deal of the drop in interest rates. As Chart 1.4 illustrates, the long-term drop in rates has closely tracked the long-term deceleration in NGDP.

This trend towards slower growth, already visible early last decade, became even more pronounced following the financial crisis. As both real economic activity and inflation fell, nominal growth hit a low not seen in more than 50 years. In this context it should not come as a surprise that interest rates are low.

Growth is low in part because investors are still paying off the excess debt accumulated during last decade's housing boom. This post-crisis hangover has arguably been inhibiting growth since the last recession. Thankfully, things have started to improve. Most households in the United States have a more manageable debt load, thanks in part to low interest rates, which make the remaining debt easier to service. Admittedly, other parts of the world, notably the UK and Canada, are still struggling with high consumer debt levels. Yet, despite the improvement in consumer balance sheets, rates remain near record lows.

Chart 1.4: US ten-year Treasury yield versus nominal GDP (%)

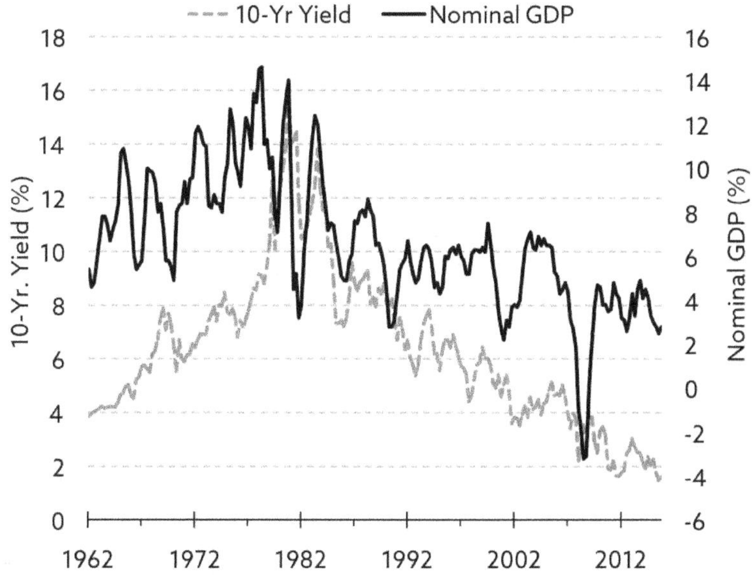

Source: Bloomberg, March 2017.

Demographic difficulties

Beyond low NGDP there are other factors at work as well. It is important to note that the trend towards lower growth and low rates began before the financial crisis. Growth, both real and nominal, has been decelerating since 2000. While most will associate that year with the bursting of the tech bubble and a brutal bear market in stocks, the date is significant for another reason as well. This was the time when demographics started to shift for the worse in many developed countries.

While the collapse in technology stocks produced a temporary loss in confidence, the recession that followed was mild by historical standards. What really changed was not the value of technology companies but the rate at which people were participating in the labor market. This marked the reversal of a multi-decade trend that had been supporting growth for most of the period since the second world war.

In the 1970s and 1980s, women began to enter the workforce in large numbers. This caused a steady rise in workforce participation – a measure of what portion of the population is engaged in the labor market. That trend reached a peak in 2000. At that time, the participation rate in the United States hit a record high of 67%. Since then the trend has been lower, with the current rate close to the lowest level since the late 1970s (see Chart 1.5). This is exerting downward pressure on growth.

The reason the slowdown in the labor force is so important is that a country's long-term potential growth rate is a function of only two things: growth in productivity and growth in hours worked. If the workforce is growing at a slower pace – or as in the case in Japan and parts of Europe, shrinking – productivity has to grow unusually fast just to keep growth positive.

While the United States has a much younger population than Japan or parts of western Europe, both population growth and workforce participation are falling. This suggests that the potential growth rate of the economy in most developed countries is substantially lower than it was 50 years ago, when the baby boomers were entering the workforce in record numbers.

Chart 1.5: US labor force participation rate (%)

Source: Bloomberg, March 2017.

The end of retail therapy?

An older workforce also exerts downward pressure on interest rates through a second transmission mechanism. As people age, their propensity to spend and save shifts. For most individuals and families, large purchases such as a home tend to occur when younger. Young families spend more, not just on homes but on home furnishings, apparel and durable goods. They also tend to borrow more to pay for those purchases.

As people age their spending habits shift. One big change is that more spending goes to healthcare. In addition, older couples will often shed the family house and move to a smaller residence. And as individuals and couples approach retirement, their financial advisors begin to shift asset allocations towards income-producing assets.

The above trends have the aggregate impact of putting downward pressure on interest rates. As people borrow less, the demand for credit is further suppressed. Simultaneously, the preference for income adds to the demand for bonds and dividend-paying stocks. As the demand for bonds goes up, so do prices. As bonds pay a fixed payment, higher prices translate into lower yields. The net effect is that the combination of lower propensity to borrow and a bigger appetite for bonds pushes real, or inflation-adjusted, interest rates lower.

As a result, there is considerable evidence that countries with older populations tend to experience lower real interest rates. Now consider the effect as most of the developed world, along with China, ages. In addition to a credit hangover, demographics help explain a significant portion of the slowdown in growth as well as the low-rate regime.

Remember inflation? Not really

We have now established that slow nominal economic growth has helped to keep interest rates unusually low. There has been another culprit as well. Remember the previous formula for nominal growth: NGDP = real growth + inflation. Low rates are not just a function of slow growth, but are also caused by few inflationary pressures in most countries.

One of the distinguishing features of the recovery since the financial crisis has been that even as the job market has improved, and oil has occasionally spiked, inflation has remained low. While certain costs, notably medical care and education, have risen, overall inflation has remained remarkably muted.

Low inflation, like slow growth, is a function of many factors. We live in an unusual time, at least relative to the 1970s, 1980s and 1990s, in that many things are getting cheaper. For example, the cost of electronics and apparel have actually been falling in recent years. The net effect is that we've been in a prolonged period of disinflation in most developed countries.

To be clear, disinflation is not the same as deflation. The former refers to downward pressure on prices, not necessarily falling prices. While few countries outside Japan have or are experiencing outright deflation, most of the developed world is experiencing low inflation, often 1%–2% or less. This is where inflation has been for much of the post-crisis period.

Sluggish growth helps explain low inflation. When demand is soft there is enough capacity to produce most goods and services and there are few bottlenecks to cause prices to rise. However, we've had previous periods of soft growth in the United States and other developed countries and inflation was much higher. The 1970s even had a name for it: stagflation. That was a period when growth was slow but inflation high.

There are several differences between the 1970s and today that help explain the lack of inflation. Demographics is certainly part of it. As discussed above, changing consumption patterns impact demand and have contributed to lower prices.

In addition to a soft economy and an aging population, shifting consumption habits among the young – think Amazon, Uber and Airbnb – have also been conspiring to keep prices down. People are spending differently than they did several decades ago. They are spending more on technology, travel and experiences, and less on goods.

One example of this trend is apparel. Overall prices for clothing – forget about luxury brands for a moment – have actually been flat to falling in recent years. Except for a brief spike in 2011 and early 2012, the price of apparel in the United States has barely been growing since 2010. During most of this period, annual inflation for apparel has been between +0.5% and –2%. In other words, for much of this period the price of clothing has actually been falling.

Another big contributor to falling prices has been technology. While not always obvious, the cost of technology has been sliding for decades. Even in those instances when we pay the same or even a bit more for a smart phone or laptop, the true price is falling rapidly given how much more these devices can do.

The increase in computing power has been so dramatic and rapid that it cannot even be measured using a normal scale. Instead, you need to think about improvements in performance on what is known as a log scale. In other words, to measure the increase in computer processing power you have to think in terms of factors of 1,000, 10,000 or even more!

Take the example of a now ubiquitous item: the iPad. Outside of a multi-million dollar mainframe computer, that much computing power did not even exist 40 years ago. Even as recently as the 1980s, the cost of that much processing would have been one thousand times what it costs today. But in 2017, a device most take for granted costs pennies relative to what you would have had to pay 30 years ago.

A more generalized example is the price of a semiconductor, the basic building block of the information age. Not only has the processing power of semiconductors expanded at an exponential rate, but the cost has been dropping for decades (see Chart 1.6). Today, electronic devices from smart phones to computers are both significantly more powerful *and* cheaper.

As the cost of computing power and data heads steadily lower, this trend will continue to exert downward pressure on large segments of the economy. Inflation will rise and fall based on cyclical shifts in demand, but a case can be made that there are powerful forces at work in the background that are holding prices down.

An aging population, changing spending patterns and the relentless upward march in technology are all having a persistent and powerful impact on inflation. Together they help explain why even in the ninth year of an economic recovery, inflation has remained so persistently and stubbornly low. This in turn has contributed to the persistence of the low-rate environment.

Chart 1.6: US producer prices – semiconductors ($)

Source: Bloomberg, April 2017.

An unlimited credit card

Apart from slow growth and low inflation there is a final, crucial reason that interest rates are as low as they are. The Federal Reserve and the other major central banks want them that way.

Following the last recession, central banks were at pains to provide economic stimulus. Most of the world's central banks were understandably fixated on preventing another Great Depression. Unfortunately, they soon ran into a problem. What do you do when rates are already at zero and the economy is still struggling?

Typically when a recession hits, central banks lower interest rates to spur demand. The problem during the Great Recession was that rates were already low when the recession began. In addition, this was the most severe downturn in the global economy since the 1930s. The world's central banks soon found themselves out of ammunition as interest rates approached zero.

Unable to lower rates any further – an obstacle the Bank of Japan and the European Central Bank ultimately overcame by demonstrating that interest rates can indeed go negative – and still facing a collapse in demand, central banks got creative. Typically central banks focus their efforts on short-term interest rates, allowing long-term rates to fluctuate with market conditions. Given the unusual nature of the financial crisis, many of the world's largest central banks made the decision to expand their toolkit.

Beginning shortly after the crisis and continuing to today in Europe and Japan, central banks began buying financial assets, primarily government bonds. They did this as the modern equivalent of creating money and the process has become known as quantitative easing (QE).

As central banks bought bonds, two things happened. First, central banks have balance sheets with assets and liabilities, similar to commercial banks. Buying bonds expanded the balance sheets of the respective central banks. Second, when the Fed or another central bank bought a bond they paid for it by debiting the account that a commercial bank had with the respective central bank.

This process resulted in both more excess reserves – reserves beyond what banks need to hold – for commercial banks and much bigger balance sheets for central banks (see Chart 1.7). By purchasing trillions of dollars' worth of bonds central banks drove up demand. This had the mechanical effect of pushing bond prices up and yields down.

Consider the effect on rates. In the United States, the United Kingdom, the euro-zone and Japan, central banks have been spending trillions of dollars, pounds, euros and yen to buy bonds. They were making these purchases with money conjured out of the financial ether and were doing so *regardless* of the price of the bonds. They were not looking for a return on investment. Instead, buying bonds was simply an extension of their traditional monetary toolkit.

Central bank buying is an entirely new source of demand. With investors facing a determined buyer with unlimited resources – the only limit on central bank buying has been that eventually they run out of bonds to buy – investors piled on and added to the frenzy. As bond prices rose, yields plummeted. As a result, bond yields reached levels that most investors thought impossible.

Chart 1.7: US Federal Reserve balance sheet ($ trillions)

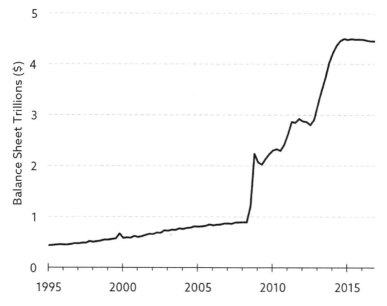

Source: Bloomberg, March 2017.

While QE has been halted in the United States, central banks in Europe and Japan continue to buy tens of billions of government bonds and other securities (see Chart 1.8). The net result is that the Bank of Japan (BOJ) and European Central Bank (ECB) have built up balance sheets that, relative to the size of their respective economies, dwarf the relatively miserly work of the Fed.

Chart 1.8: Bank of Japan balance sheet (% GDP)

Source: Bloomberg, April 2017.

Bond market refugees

Economists will debate for decades whether QE was justified, effective or even legal. What is clearer is that trillions of dollars spent on bonds has contributed to the drop in interest rates. Pushing interest rates down to unprecedented levels has had, and continues to have, a profound impact on investor behavior.

All across the developed world investors have had to adjust to a scenario in which income-generating assets are suddenly scarce. In some instances, investors simply accepted a lower return. More often they looked elsewhere, taking on more risk in the process. By driving interest rates to absurdly low levels, central banks have created an unexpected dilemma for investors, particularly those investing for income: what do you do when traditional bonds no longer pay a reasonable rate of interest?

The simple answer is you look for other things to buy, even at the cost of more risk. If bonds are no longer paying a reasonable level of income, more adventurous investors turn to an increasingly broad set of alternatives. These can include everything from dividend-paying stocks to real estate to oil pipelines.

Regardless of the particular instrument, the one clear trend has been that other assets have become more expensive. As investors have stretched for income, they have pushed up the valuation of these assets. The net result is that many of these instruments, often referred to as *bond market proxies*, produce far less income and trade at a much higher valuation than was the case a decade ago.

This phenomenon is evident in many corners of the market. In particular, it is evident when looking at how defensive stocks in the United States have been trading. Defensive stocks are relatively safe companies that pay a high, steady dividend. Examples could include food and beverage firms, such as Nestlé, or utility companies, such as Duke Energy. They are often found in established industries, such as utilities, food and tobacco.

There was a time when demand for these securities mostly came from retirees, more conservative investors and those occasionally looking for a safe port during a financial meltdown. Today the list of buyers has grown as investors look for bond market substitutes.

Unfortunately, buying stocks that pay a dividend is not a complete solution that comes without consequences. The first challenge is that, as with bonds, the low-rate environment has pushed up valuations. As investors have increasingly turned to these securities – investors buying them even have a name, *bond market refugees* – valuations have risen even as yields have fallen.

The high price of income

This rise in valuations of income-producing securities makes little sense, until you control for the drop in interest rates. US utility companies provide an excellent example of how the drop in bond yields has reverberated throughout financial markets.

Most traditional utility companies are slow-growing, regulated businesses. They have been and still are considerably less profitable than the typical US-listed company. They have also historically traded at a lower valuation than faster growing companies or the broader stock market.

For example, from 1995 to the end of 2004, the price-to-earnings ratio (P/E) for the S&P 500 Utility Sector traded at around a 35% discount to the broader US stock market. If the S&P 500 was trading at a P/E ratio of 20, the utility sector would typically trade at a P/E closer to 15 or 16. Their multiple to the market was typically less than one.

Since the financial crisis, US utility companies have been trading differently – they have tended to trade at a smaller discount to the market. Chart 1.9 shows the historic pattern and how things have changed recently. Again, it is not the case that utility companies have magically become better businesses. They are still the same, somewhat boring but steady companies.

Instead, the shift in valuation is a function of the change in the rate environment. In a world in which a 3% or 4% yield is increasingly hard to come by, investors are more willing to pay a premium to get what is considered a *safe* yield. The downside of this strategy is that when rates do occasionally go back up, these stocks often perform worse than the broader market.

The second challenge – beyond rising valuations – involves the volatility of these securities. While many dividend-paying stocks tend to be less volatile than the average stock, they are still more volatile than bonds. This is because even lower-risk stocks tend to be much more volatile than a bond, particularly a safe government bond of the type investors used to rely on for income. In the name of generating income, investors have willingly – or unwittingly – accepted additional volatility. For some, this may not be a good idea.

Chart 1.9: Relative value of the S&P 500 Utility Sector

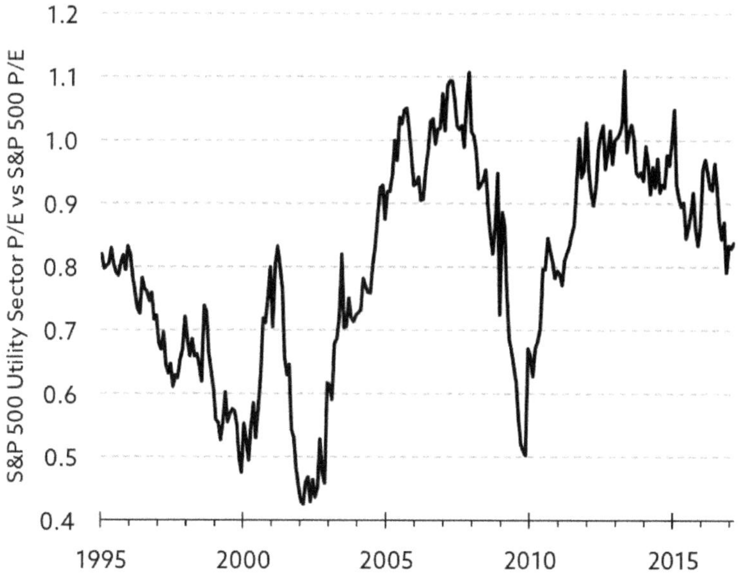

Source: Bloomberg, March 2017.

As most investors have a limited appetite for risk, buying riskier securities as a substitute for safer ones does not always end well. Bonds have traditionally helped to dampen the higher volatility of stocks. If investors turn to bond market substitutes, such as dividend-paying stocks, they will generate some additional income. However, that additional income will come at the cost of more volatility.

For those unaware of the trade-off they may be in for a nasty surprise when volatility rises, particularly if it rises because interest rates are heading higher. Under this scenario, safe defensive stocks may not seem so safe.

Low rates change everything

Interest rates set the tone for all assets. What you pay for money in turn influences what you will pay for everything else. This includes houses, cars, stocks or even an ounce of gold.

The unprecedented drop in interest rates has multiples causes, ranging from slow growth, to changing demographics to central bank policy. Some of these factors will fade over time, notably central bank support. Others, including demographics and the deflationary impact of technology, are likely to be with us for years if not decades.

This suggests that even when rates rise, which they are likely to do as central banks pull back, the rise will be modest. The takeaway is that a low, and somewhat more volatile, rate environment presents a unique set of challenges for anyone trying to build a portfolio. The most obvious challenge is a lack of income. The less obvious challenges can be just as impactful on a portfolio.

Bond duration: low rates = more risk

If dividend-paying stocks and other bond market proxies are both expensive and more volatile, should investors simply accept less income and maintain their traditional exposure to bonds? This is probably the correct answer for the more conservative, but it still leaves investors with a problem.

As discussed previously, in addition to income, bonds mitigate overall portfolio volatility. Bonds' ability to dampen portfolio volatility is a function of two characteristics: lower overall volatility and a low, and often negative, correlation with stocks. Both characteristics are now more questionable.

Even riskier bonds, such as high-yield bonds, typically carry less volatility than most stocks. That is because the income on bonds is more reliable. Governments generally pay their bills. While not unheard of – think Greece – developed governments rarely default on their debts.

While corporate issuers do default, the bondholder has more rights than the equity holder. The holder of a company's bonds has a higher claim on that company's assets, affording some protection. This is why bonds are considered the safer of the two main building blocks in a portfolio.

However, while bondholders typically get paid at maturity, a lot of things can happen in the interim. Bond prices change, often abruptly, with market conditions. There is a set of circumstances when bond volatility can rise abruptly. This is when interest rates are rising unexpectedly.

As traditional bonds offer fixed interest payments, the value of those payments declines when interest rates rise. While a bond will pay its full face value at maturity, its current value moves up or down depending on the prevailing level of interest rates. This sensitivity to interest rates is known as a bond's duration. The higher the duration, the more sensitive it is, i.e. the more bonds will decline when interest rates rise.

Longer-term bonds have longer durations as investors have to wait longer to get back their initial investment. One way to think about this is that the duration represents the weighted average of future cash flows. As an example, consider two bonds, both maturing in ten years, but one with a 3% annual yield and the other with a 6% yield. The holder of the second bond, with the 6% yield, will get back more money prior to maturity. As a result, even though both bonds mature in ten years, the bond with the 3% yield has a higher duration and is more sensitive to rising rates.

This much is standard math. What has changed is that the low-rate regime has pushed down rates across the entire bond universe. This has had the mechanical effect of pushing durations higher for most bonds and bond funds. An investor in a typical bond mutual fund has to contend with lower yield *and* higher duration (see Chart 1.10).

Up until recently, investors have benefited from duration, or sensitivity to interest rates. Lower rates have pushed up the value of most bonds. However, after hitting an historic low in July 2016, it is not clear that this multi-decade bull market in bonds will continue. While rates are unlikely to surge, even a small rise in rates can inflict losses on bonds, or more to the point more significant losses than investors have become accustomed to.

Chart 1.10: The duration of the ten-year Barclays US Treasury index – a bellwether for longer-term bonds

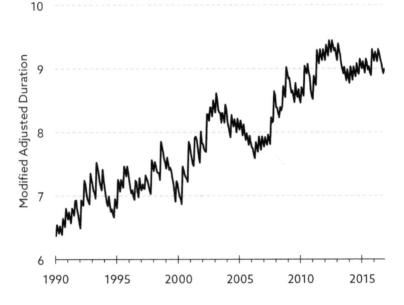

Source: Bloomberg, March 2017.

Getting in sync

There is a final complication related to bonds. While rates have been low and durations high for a number of years, bonds have still been a reliable portfolio diversifier. More specifically, they have helped to diversify risk from the equity portion of a portfolio.

Since before the financial crisis, bonds have tended to be negatively correlated with stocks. This has been true even when bonds were the *source* of the volatility, as was the case during the US debt downgrade in 2011. In that instance investors were contending with an unprecedented downgrade of US debt. That should have sent them scurrying *away* from US government debt. Instead, bond prices rose and rates fell as investors instead decided that the bigger threat to their portfolios was a massive sell-off in stocks.

From this and similar episodes, investors developed an almost childlike faith in the diversifying benefits of bonds. The lesson being: even when bonds are the source of volatility they are still the place to hide.

And for most of the past five or ten years that faith has been rewarded. Bonds have provided a reliable hedge. That said, investors need to remind themselves that this is not necessarily a permanent state of affairs.

Looking at many decades of stock and bond returns, over the long term stocks and bonds have historically had a zero, rather than a negative correlation (a correlation of +1 indicates perfect co-movement while a correlation of −1 indicates that the two assets co-move perfectly, but in opposite directions).

Over the long term, not only have stock/bond correlations averaged zero, there have been numerous periods when stocks and bonds have been *positively* correlated (see Chart 1.11). During these periods, holding bonds and stocks together would magnify rather than reduce losses.

Chart 1.11: US stock-bond correlation

Source: Bloomberg, March 2017.

Regime shift?

Typically these periods of positive stocks/bond correlations have occurred when investors are concerned about the Fed. More specifically, stocks and bonds have tended towards higher correlations when monetary conditions are tighter, with tighter being defined as higher short-term rates.

In contrast, the recent environment has been characterized by fears about growth, not rates. Investors have accurately predicted that central bank policy would remain ultra-accommodative. Instead, most bouts of investor anxiety have centered on economic or political risk, not tighter monetary policy. It is precisely during these periods when stocks and bonds are most likely to be negatively correlated. When everyone is preoccupied with a growth shock or recession, bonds are typically the best place to hide.

Ironically, to the extent a marginally better economy causes the Fed and other central banks to contemplate tightening, this may change this comfortable arrangement. There have been at least two incidents in recent years – early 2013 and late 2016 – when stock/bond correlations have risen. Both periods involved worries over the Fed tightening monetary conditions.

As of early 2017, that process was solidly under way, with the potential for further tightening in coming years. Not only is the Fed likely to continue to push short-term interest rates higher, but at some point they will start to reduce their enormous balance sheet. This may happen simply through allowing existing bonds in their inventory to mature and not reinvesting the proceeds. At the same time, other central banks, notably the ECB, are starting to contemplate the end of their own QE programs.

When central banks start to tighten, the risks to investors become more symmetrical. Now investors have something to keep them up at night other than the next recession. They become afraid of tighter monetary conditions, which have often preceded bear markets. A world in which investors rediscover a healthy fear of central banks is one in which bonds may be a less reliable hedge.

It's not all about returns

At first, changing stock/bond correlations seem like a second-order, somewhat geeky thing to worry about. Interest rates are low and stock valuations are elevated. Aren't there bigger problems than how much stocks and bonds tend to move together?

Not to dismiss all of the other challenges, this is an issue that merits some attention. For most portfolios, equities account for most of the risk. Even if stocks are only 50% of a portfolio, given that stocks are much more volatile than bonds they will account for most of the overall portfolio risk (I explore this in more detail in Chapter 3).

How to hedge that risk is crucial for any investor that is unwilling to experience the full volatility of equity markets. To the extent that bonds are a less reliable way to manage volatility, this is a game changer. The challenge is of course only compounded by a lack of income from bonds and longer durations.

Given these challenges, investors are going to need to contemplate some changes to the way they build portfolios. These include considering portfolios with different assets and a broader range of geographies. It also suggests a greater focus on risk management.

But before getting into the specifics, it is worth taking a step back to establish first principles. As discussed in the introduction, before considering the financial landscape investors need to start with their own needs and limitations, which is what we move on to in the next chapter.

Key concepts

- Rates are exceptionally low throughout most of the world.
- Low rates are a function of several factors. Some factors, notably central bank buying, may fade over time. Others, including secular forces holding down growth and inflation, are less likely to change. This suggests rates are likely to remain low relative to historic levels.
- The search for yield has driven up valuations in many asset classes. Higher valuations typically equate with lower returns over the next

five to ten years. The list of asset classes with extended valuations includes many income-producing assets, such as high-yield bonds and dividend-paying stocks.

➥ Low rates have also pushed up the duration on most bonds and bond funds. Higher durations put traditional bonds at risk. They will experience larger than typical losses when rates rise.

➥ When and if monetary policy normalizes, this may impact the extent to which bonds provide diversification. Under these conditions, investors face the additional complication of a riskier portfolio.

2

Investment Therapy: Setting Objectives, Removing Constraints

WHEN BUILDING A portfolio, the natural inclination is to start with the markets. It makes intuitive sense that a portfolio should first and foremost reflect investment views. What is expected from stocks, bonds and other asset classes? That is, after all, what ultimately drives a portfolio. While true, this ignores a preliminary but crucial step.

Before making market prognostications, investors and their advisors need to first look inward. The first step in the investment process has nothing to do with the economy, interest rates or equity valuations. Investing starts with a goal and a set of clear objectives.

Thus, a well-constructed portfolio is built around a goal and constraints. The goal defines the objective, for example total return or income. The constraints define self-imposed limits, such as not buying commodities or having a limit on risk. In practice, these parameters, more than any single market view, define the broad contours of a portfolio.

To many, talking about defining investment objectives seems redundant, bordering on silly. Isn't the point of investing simply to make money? The problem is, defining an investment objective as simply "making money" ignores several issues: how much money, when it is needed and, most importantly, what risks is the investor willing to take?

While the obvious answer to the first question is "as much as possible", the unfortunate fact is that it is difficult to make more money in financial markets without taking more risk. An investor looking to produce double digit returns must be prepared to take an enormous amount of risk. This was always true but becomes even more unavoidable in a world in which cash pays close to nothing (see Chapter 1).

In the current environment, generating even low-to-mid single digit returns requires taking risk, some of which may not be obvious. As a result, even more than usual investors need a clear plan, specific objectives and enumerated constraints. These areas are the focus of this chapter.

The objective

The first step in the investment process is specifying the investor's preference on when they want the money. Put differently, is the main goal long-term growth, or is the investor looking for current income. For many, the answer is a bit of both.

This chapter will focus on setting the portfolio's objective. Later in the book, mostly in Chapter 7, I delve into more detail on how that objective is translated into an actual portfolio. But before thinking about implementation, investors need to be explicit as to the goal of the portfolio. At a very high level, this normally breaks down to some combination of income versus total return.

Classic financial theory suggests that investors should be indifferent to the source of their return; they can always sell some of their portfolio, thereby creating an income stream. However, the simple fact is that most investors have a strong preference for one form of return over another.

To the extent an investor is primarily concerned with income (dividends or interest), this will lead to a very different portfolio than one focused on total return (capital appreciation plus dividends or interest). A portfolio tilted towards income will tend to hold more bonds and dividend-paying stocks and potentially more niche assets such as preferred stocks or Master Limited Partnerships (MLPs). Assets that may produce high growth but little income, such as emerging market (EM) equities, are likely to be of less interest. An EM stock may double over the next couple of years, but if it provides no immediate income it doesn't necessarily align with the goals of an income-oriented investor.

This is a critical point. While an income investor may be very bullish on gold, that asset offers no income. While a small amount of gold may be desirable to help diversify the portfolio, the amount the investor holds will be limited by the simple fact that the asset is not aligned with the portfolio's objective. In contrast, if the objective is total return, the process should favor assets with high expected total return, regardless of whether or not they produce any income.

The objective of the investor therefore determines the allocation as much as any other consideration. In other words, how you prioritize growth, income or other objectives, such as socially responsible investing, will broadly define the shape of your portfolio. If you prioritize income, your portfolio will by definition have more bonds and dividend-paying stocks than a growth-oriented portfolio. To demonstrate, it is worth looking at the income objective in a little more detail.

Income: blood from a stone

As discussed in the previous chapter, building a portfolio dedicated to income has become an increasingly difficult endeavor. Prior to the financial crisis it was relatively simple. Many retirees either bought an annuity or they could construct an annuity themselves through a common practice known as a bond ladder.

Those looking for a bit more income also had alternatives. A more aggressive investor could add high-yield or emerging market bonds. Even without taking much risk, it was not particularly difficult to build a portfolio that generated 4%–5% annual income.

Today, the number of bonds yielding more than 4% is less than 20% of the overall bond market. Of the few remaining bonds left that do pay more than 4%, all entail considerable risk. Many are more exotic than most investors are used to – think government debt from Greece or bonds from a distressed energy company. Building a bond ladder out of traditional bonds is still possible, but it will produce a much reduced income stream. Today, if you want higher income you need to take significantly more risk. This challenge is even greater if you frame the problem in terms of inflation-adjusted returns, also referred to as real returns.

Getting a high nominal return feels nice. Today, many can only dream about the eye-watering yields of the early 1980s, when even short-term government debt was yielding over 10%. What is missing from the financial nostalgia is inflation.

In the summer of 1980, an investor could still buy a 10-year US government bond yielding more than 10%. Sounds fantastic, except for the fact that inflation was running at around 14%. It's no good to get a large, fixed return if inflation will erode the real purchasing power of the income.

Now, in retrospect, buying that bond at a 10% or 11% yield was a phenomenal investment. Inflation soon started to plunge and with it interest rates. Anyone with the foresight to buy that bond received a double digit, tax advantaged and safe return throughout the following decade.

The challenge today is that not only are bond yields low in an absolute sense, but, as was the case in the early 1980s, the yield is often below the level of inflation. This means that investors are receiving little to no real return. To add insult to injury, unlike in the early 1980s when inflation had a good way to fall, it is less likely to drop today. This means that investors may be stuck with not only a low nominal yield but a very poor real one as well.

This matters a great deal. Investors need to consider the impact of inflation when contemplating a multi-decade retirement. It is not enough to just generate income. That income has to be worth enough to support the investor's spending needs as inflation rises, even if it is rising very slowly. Inflation at 2% sounds modest, until you consider the impact of compounding over a multi-decade period. Over a two-decade period, a realistic time frame for most new retirees, a 2% annualized inflation rate would result in nearly a 50% increase in the cost of living.

Low real yields have been a problem for a long time, but the situation has gotten worse in recent years. Prior to the financial crisis, real bond yields typically averaged 2% or more. Even in countries like Japan, where nominal yields were and are abnormally low, the after-inflation return was consistently above zero and often more than 2%. Today, in much of Europe interest rates are still flirting with negative territory. For example, see Chart 2.1, which traces the path of the Swiss 10-year bond yield since 1988.

Chart 2.1: Swiss 10-year bond yield (%)

Source: Bloomberg, April 2017.

Nor is the solution to low yields to simply buy riskier bonds. Even for investors willing to invest in corporate bonds, which carry some risk of default, options are limited. As investors have migrated out of safer government bonds in search of yield, this has pushed the price of corporate bonds higher, and their yields lower.

As Chart 2.2 illustrates, while yields have been falling for decades, the process has reached a critical juncture in recent years. Bond yields are now at levels last seen several generations ago.

The Moody's Baa Index tracks the yield on the lower part of the investment grade bond spectrum. Bond issues in this category come with some risk of default. Despite that risk, in the spring of 2017 the yield available on a broad index of these bonds was only 4.5% (see Chart 2.2). By comparison, the 50-year average is approximately 8.50%.

Chart 2.2: Yield-to-maturity, Moody's Baa Bond Index (%)

Source: Bloomberg, April 2017.

The takeaway is that income has become an extremely scarce commodity. Investors focused on income generation have two somewhat stark choices: accept more risk or less income. For those looking for a third way, it may be more prudent to focus on total return with an eye towards income rather than making income the sole objective.

For the remainder of the book, I use the example of a portfolio focused on total return. But for those focused on income, the same rules regarding risk, return and portfolio construction still apply. The only difference being that your return assumptions are expressed in terms of expected income, rather than total return.

Unavoidable risk

The next chapter will define and discuss portfolio risk. That said, it is important to briefly introduce one definition of risk here, in order to highlight a key point: portfolio objectives need to take risk into consideration. Everybody wants higher returns; not everybody is willing to take more risk.

This is why investors should become familiar with the concept of a risk budget. If the first question for any investor is when they want their money – income or growth – the second needs to be how much risk they're willing to accept. Think of the risk budget as the amount of risk the investor is willing to spend in order to reach their goals. Put differently, the risk budget defines the outer limit of how much risk the investor is willing to take.

The question of when and where to accept risk raises the question of what risks we're talking about in the first place. There are, after all, different sources of risk. Some risk can be diversified away by buying different types of securities or assets. This type of risk is known as *specific* or *idiosyncratic risk*.

If you don't believe you have any particular skill in picking stocks or bonds, and assuming you're skeptical that anyone else can do it any better, your goal is to eliminate or at least minimize idiosyncratic risk. The easiest way to limit idiosyncratic risk is to own a broad, well diversified mutual fund or ETF.

While an investor can limit their exposure to the risk of any one stock or bond, some risks can't be diversified away. Investors looking to do better than the paltry returns on cash need to be in the market. That entails unavoidable risk: the *market risk*.

In considering market risk it is useful to think about the returns to different types of assets. At the most conservative end of the spectrum is cash. Cash can be eroded by inflation over time, but in the short term there is no risk to holding cash. This is why cash, or a cash equivalent such as a short-term government bond, is referred to as the risk-free asset.

The return to the risk-free asset is the starting point. This is what the investor gets if they are unwilling to do anything that entails either market risk or liquidity risk, i.e. the risk that you can't get your money whenever you want it. The risk-free rate is an important concept in finance as it sets the stage for every subsequent financial decision.

Any investment that entails risk needs to provide an expected return that is greater than that offered by the risk-free asset. Otherwise, nobody would be incentivized to do anything other than hold cash. Investors looking for a higher return, which includes just about everybody not rich enough to live off the interest on their checking account, needs to accept some marginal risk above the risk-free rate.

Risk versus return: look for a steep line

The potential return for taking incremental risk is of course unknowable in advance. There are times when investors would have been better off keeping their money in cash. At other times, such as buying a Treasury bond in 1980, the return to an asset turned out to be well above any reasonable expectations.

While investors will never know the actual return in advance, there are a few safe assumptions you can make. Over the long term – defined as a period of ten years or more – the return to broad asset classes, such as different types of stocks and bonds, generally scales with risk. The more risk, the higher the potential return.

This is why stocks, which are inherently more risky than bonds, typically produce higher returns over the long term. If they didn't, why would anyone accept the risk of losing money in stocks when they could just buy a relatively safe Treasury bond or Gilt?

One way to consider how much potential return the investor can generate is to plot the return expected from various asset classes against their risk (see Chart 2.3). Whenever you do this exercise, the *line* that describes the relationship between risk and return should slope upward and to the right. This is consistent with the notion of more return for each additional unit of risk (there is more on how to actually measure risk in the next chapter).

Investors need to also pay attention to the slope, or steepness, of the line. When the slope of the line is steep, meaning the line is rising faster, investors are potentially rewarded for taking more risk. The steeper the line, the greater the potential reward. However, when the slope is shallow this is telling you something important: riskier assets don't provide much in the way of incremental return. Unfortunately, that is the position we find ourselves in today. As to why, thank central banks.

Low rates have pushed normally conservative investors out of safe assets, like cash and government bonds. As investors have been starved of income, they have piled into riskier assets, such as high-yield bonds and stocks. The cumulative impact of this multi-year trend has been to push valuations up. To the extent valuations are now higher than normal for most bonds and US stocks, future returns are likely to be lower.

For investors this suggests that today, risk is not rewarded to the same extent it typically has been for past generations of investors. This doesn't suggest taking no risk, but does imply that this is not the most opportune time to aggressively stretch for either yield or overall portfolio return.

Chart 2.3: Theoretical long-term risk and return estimates

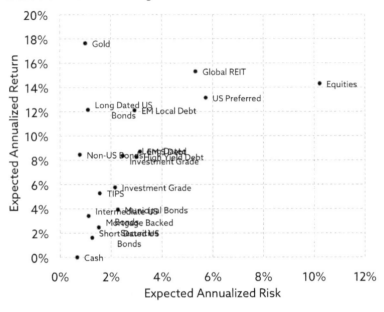

Asset	Return	Risk
Cash	0.67%	0.00%
Gold	1.00%	17.64%
Non-U.S Bonds	0.78%	8.47%
Long Dated US Bonds	1.10%	12.15%
Intermediate US Bonds	1.12%	3.41%
Short-Dated US Bonds	1.26%	1.61%
Mortgage Backed Securities	1.52%	2.48%
TIPS	1.56%	5.28%
Investment Grade	2.16%	5.76%
Municipal Bonds	2.27%	3.94%
Long Dated Investment Grade	2.46%	8.38%
EM Local Debt	2.93%	12.11%
High-Yield Debt	3.00%	8.28%
EM $ Debt	3.14%	8.72$
Global REIT	5.32%	15.32%
U.S. Preferred	5.72%	13.15%
Equities	10.22%	14.31%

Source: BlackRock, Global Allocation, April 2017.

Constraints: the ties that bind

The first obstacle to the nirvana of high returns is risk. This is always the biggest challenge and the one to which the entire next chapter is devoted. Aside from risk, most investors have other limitations. Many relate indirectly to risk.

For example, some investors avoid stocks from emerging markets, such as China or Brazil. This decision may in part be driven by risk considerations; these markets are riskier than those of the US or UK. In some cases, the aversion is less about risk and more about a lack of familiarity.

Regardless of the precise reason, investors need to be very aware of the limitations they put on their portfolios. An unwillingness to buy emerging market stocks is a typical example of a constraint. As with the objective and risk budget, constraints have a profound impact on the shape of a portfolio.

Expanding on the above example, constraints take different forms. They may be at the security level, such as an unwillingness to buy alcohol or tobacco stocks, or at the asset class level. A typical example of the latter would be an investor unwilling to buy gold or other precious metals.

Some constraints are practical. For many individual investors, tax law creates some very reasonable constraints. In the United States it is not uncommon for investors to exclude any type of investment that generates a K-1, a tax form for certain types of investment holdings. Most investors hate K-1s because they often result in having to delay annual tax filings. For these investors, the marginal return available from these investments is simply not worth the administrative hassle of having to delay filing their taxes.

However, while tax considerations are a valid constraint, others are less so. This can be an issue. As a general rule, an investor should question his or her constraints and limit them wherever possible.

One of the most common types of constraints has to do with investing internationally. Many if not most investors impose a limit on how much of their portfolio they are willing to invest in a country outside their own. Often the limit is zero; they won't buy international stocks or bonds.

An unwillingness to invest outside of one's home country is known as a home country bias. It is one of the more dangerous constraints and one that should be avoided whenever possible.

The reluctant tourist

I return to the process of building a portfolio in more detail in Chapter 7, but for now let's take a simple example of how certain constraints can limit a portfolio. Imagine a conservative US-based investor who is worried about the riskiness of stocks. He is particularly worried about non-US stocks. As a result, he is unwilling to hold more than 25% of his portfolio in equities and will not invest outside of the United States.

If you try to design a portfolio to maximize returns for this investor you'll soon hit a wall. Even if in theory you're willing to take lots of risk, the equity-related constraints dramatically restrict where the portfolio can be invested, and by extension the portfolio's return potential.

Chart 2.4 illustrates what a theoretical portfolio with these constraints might look like. It was built using mean variance optimization (MVO), a method designed to balance both risk and return (more about MVO in Chapter 7).

The dual constraint around equities in general and non-US equities in particular results in a portfolio that is 85% invested in US stocks, high-yield and emerging market debt. This is a very concentrated portfolio. By limiting international investments you wind up buying other assets that might not be that additive, either because they don't produce much in the way of incremental return or they add unnecessary risk.

The constraint on equities in general and international equities in particular introduces another problem. Much like a game of whack-a-mole, you constrain one part of a portfolio only to see risk pop up somewhere else. By limiting international equities, the portfolio construction process was driven towards the next best thing: international bonds.

Chart 2.4: Asset allocation with 25% equity limit

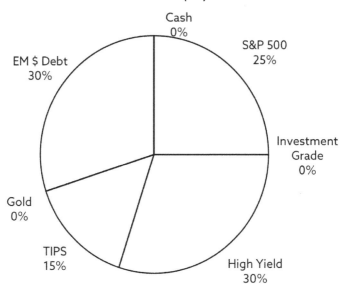

Source: Bloomberg, April 2017.

In this example, emerging market debt and high-yield bonds take the place of international stocks. This illustrates an important concept. A formal portfolio construction process, such as optimization, will look to buy assets that best meet the investor's goals, i.e. return.

If the process is prevented from buying what it perceives to be the best solution, it will then look for the next best thing. In the process of excluding some asset classes, the investor invariably winds up piling into similar ones that are not constrained. The result is too much concentration in assets that might be just as risky as the ones that were excluded.

The problem with a home country bias

Geographic constraints are always a problem. They involve limiting large chunks of the world. Even for US investors whose domestic market is the biggest and most liquid stock market in the world, they are still eliminating most of the world from their opportunity set if they restrict themselves to the US only.

Even the United States only comprises roughly 50% of the value of the global stock market (see Chart 2.5). Based on other metrics, the percentage gets much lower. The United States represents only about 5% of the world's population and accounts for between 20%–25% of global economic activity.

Chart 2.5: MSCWI All-Country World Index (ACWI)

Country	Weight (%)
United States	52.05%
Japan	7.64%
United Kingdom	5.08%
China	3.29%
Canada	3.23%
Switzerland	3.14%
France	3.12%
Germany	2.99%
Australia	2.49%
Netherlands	1.62%
South Korea	1.59%
Taiwan	1.33%
Ireland	1.23%
Other	11.20%

Source: BlackRock iShares, March 2017.

Some would argue that you don't need to leave your home country to get exposure to the rest of the world. Leading global companies sell throughout the world, so by definition you're getting exposure to the global economy when you own large, export-oriented firms.

While it is true that investors can gain access to international markets by investing in large exporters, this is not the same as international exposure. For starters, some economies, notably the US, are very domestically oriented. Buying an index of US companies, even including large global firms, most of the economic exposure will still be to the United States.

Second, owning a company or index of companies located in a different country is very different than owning a domestic company that sells abroad. The risk characteristics are different. There are different exposures to different business cycles. In short, exporters and international diversification are not fungible.

And to the extent a home country bias is a problem for US investors, with a big, diversified market, it is an even bigger problem for investors outside the United States. For starters, no other country comes close in terms of stock market capitalization (see again Chart 2.5).

Concentrated markets

Other large, developed countries such as the United Kingdom or Japan have stock markets that account for less than 10% of the global total. For investors outside the United States, a home country bias means giving up exposure to the overwhelming majority of global economic activity and global companies.

Beyond what you are giving up, a home country bias can also result in an unhealthy concentration in relatively small segments of the market. Many stock markets are dominated by a few companies or a limited number of sectors. Focusing too much of your portfolio in one country can unduly concentrate your holdings in particular types of stocks. This can lead to excessive and unnecessary risk.

A good example of this is Switzerland. Switzerland is an exceptionally wealthy country with a high standard of living. It has a world-class banking sector, global firms and a liquid, actively traded currency. However, there are lots of industries that are simply not indigenous to Switzerland. There are few energy firms or large technology companies.

Instead, the Swiss stock market is dominated by a relatively small number of companies, primarily in banking, pharmaceuticals and consumer staples (see Chart 2.6). A Swiss investor who limits her portfolio to domestic securities is not only losing out on international stocks, she is also losing out on all the industries not represented in the Swiss market. If technology or energy companies are doing well, she will not benefit. If pharmaceutical companies or banks are having a bad year, she will be disproportionately and unnecessarily hurt, relative to those holding more diversified portfolios.

The same holds for investors in Canada or Australia. These are markets with lots of natural resource companies, such as miners and large banks. But they have few global healthcare firms and fewer still tech companies. An investor that limits himself to these countries has to hope that financial and natural resource companies are always performing well. In the inevitable years when these segments trail the market, the investor will not be receiving the benefits of a more diversified portfolio.

Chart 2.6: MSCI Switzerland Index

Sector	Weight (%)
Healthcare	31.02%
Consumer Staples	20.77%
Financials	18.15%
Industrials	10.51%
Materials	9.97%
Consumer Discretionary	6.02%
Telecommunications	1.21%
Real Estate	0.77%
Other	1.58%

Source: iShares, March 2017.

Gold aversion

A home country bias refers to the practice of eliminating or limiting segments of an asset class. What about those instances when investors limit an entire asset class? Gold provides a good example of the latter.

Economists and investors from John Maynard Keynes to Warren Buffett have questioned the value and point of gold. To many it is simply an anachronism of a now defunct monetary system. Others are confused by what gold actually is. Is it a commodity like oil or copper? Not really, as there is little industrial or practical need for gold. Is it a currency like the dollar or yen? Sort of.

As a result, it is not entirely clear what gold does and why investors should own any. Not unreasonably, many decide to avoid the asset class entirely.

This arguably misses the point of what gold is, at least in the concept of a broad portfolio. Gold is, at least much of the time, a diversifier. Gold has a tendency to go up when most other asset classes are going down. In more formal terms, in most environments it has a low or even a negative correlation with financial assets, such as stocks or corporate bonds. When things are going wrong for stocks and bonds, gold is often at its best.

To illustrate, it is worth examining gold's performance during periods of market stress. In order to do this, I will introduce a measure of market volatility, the VIX Index. The VIX measures volatility in the US stock market. High readings indicate market stress while lower readings suggest a calm, generally appreciating market.

The average level of the VIX has varied with time. Over the long term, since the inception of the VIX in 1990, the index has averaged around 20. More recently, the VIX has been lower as easy money in the wake of the financial crisis has arguably suppressed market volatility (see Chart 2.7). But regardless of the average level, a rising VIX is mostly associated with rising risk aversion among investors.

Chart 2.7: The VIX Index

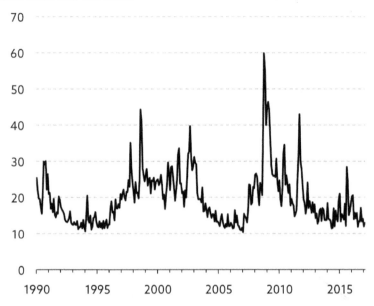

Source: Bloomberg, March 2017.

Looking back at history, the relative performance of stocks versus gold has tended to be correlated with changes in market volatility. During normal market conditions, gold generally underperforms stocks, often by quite a wide margin. However, the relationship flips when the market is under stress, indicated by a rising VIX. This relationship is particularly strong when volatility is rising rapidly.

As seen in Chart 2.8, gold typically underperforms stocks by a large margin when the VIX is down more than 25% in a month. During these periods, stocks outperform gold by an average of nearly 6% a month, a very wide margin. Even during more gentle declines in volatility, stocks reliably beat gold.

However, the pattern reverses when volatility is rising. A modest rise in the VIX suggests that gold is likely to outperform stocks. During these months, gold beats stocks by a modest 1%.

What is more striking is how gold does when volatility is rising sharply, defined as periods when volatility is up more than 25% in a given month. It is during these periods of market stress when gold proves its worth. During these months gold has beaten the S&P 500 by an average of approximately 5% a month.

Chart 2.8: VIX and monthly relative return, gold vs S&P 500, based on monthly changes in VIX, S&P 500 and spot gold (1990–present)

VIX	S&P 500 vs Gold
Down 25% or more	−5.81%
Down 25% flat	−1.90%
Flat to Up 25%	1.04%
Up 25% or more	5.06%

Source: Bloomberg, March 2017.

When markets are under extreme stress, investors tend to look for a safe port in the storm. The challenge is that when markets are selling off, there is a very short list of assets that are considered safe. This is particularly true when and if the source of the volatility is systemic, which is likely to impact the entire financial system.

During times like these the list of perceived safe assets often dwindles down to gold, US Treasuries or perhaps the Swiss franc or yen. They are considered safe havens because during these periods they are often the only asset classes that are rising. Having some allocation to safe haven assets, including gold, is an effective insurance policy during times of market stress.

Portfolio insurance

At this point some will object that if a portfolio includes safe haven bonds, such as US Treasuries, why bother with gold? Isn't that after all the point of keeping low-yielding Treasuries in a portfolio? As it turns out, gold still adds value, even if you have a significant exposure to other safe havens, such as Treasury Bonds.

Consider two portfolios. The first portfolio is a typical US long-term asset allocation: 60% US large cap equities and 40% US Treasury and other investment grade bonds. This portfolio returned around 6.25% annualized between February 2007 and December 2016. The annualized risk was a little below 9%.

Compare the performance of that portfolio to a second portfolio, one that includes a 10% weight to gold. The gold position is funded by a 5% reduction in the equity holdings and a 5% reduction in the bond holdings. The new portfolio is 55% US large cap stocks, 35% US Bonds and 10% gold. During the same time period the second portfolio produced slightly higher returns with around 0.25% less risk.

To state the obvious, the fact that gold was additive in the past does not mean it will be additive going forward. Gold prices have declined for prolonged periods, notably in the 1980s and 1990s. If interest rates rise sharply, gold is likely to lose money rather than provide a hedge.

All of those caveats aside, there is evidence that a small position in gold can help balance a portfolio during periods of market stress. This is important as it is precisely during these periods when investors are most often tempted to sell stocks and other risky assets; a decision that is almost always wrong in hindsight. Having some gold in the portfolio can help smooth the ride, thereby lessening the temptation to sell stocks near the bottom.

Emerging market phobia

The previous example focused on the loss of a hedge, something that helps mitigate downside risk. Other constraints hit returns. While investors lose an effective form of portfolio insurance by excluding gold, they may be forgoing a potential source of above-average growth by excluding emerging markets.

Earlier in the chapter I highlighted the dangers inherent in a home country bias. A more subtle version of this habit is an avoidance of emerging markets. Even for investors willing to invest in other developed regions, such as Europe or the US, many still avoid having any direct exposure to stocks or bonds listed in emerging countries such as China, India or Brazil.

Concerns about emerging markets (EMs) are neither irrational nor unwarranted. There are a host of reasons to avoid these assets. Companies in emerging countries tend to have more lax accounting standards and corporate governance. This suggests that investors can be less sure of the accounting information they are receiving. In certain countries, even basic rules of property rights are less rigorously enforced.

Apart from corporate governance and legal issues, there are a number of economic considerations. These economies are more prone to booms and busts, including massive swings in inflation. The currencies of these countries can often by quite volatile. To the extent an investor owns stocks or bonds without a currency hedge – a strategy to neutralize the impact of currency fluctuations on returns – the movement in the currency can overwhelm the return in the underlying stock or bond.

Given both the foreign exchange contribution to volatility as well as the more volatile nature of these economies, emerging market investments are typically more volatile overall than investments in developed markets. For more conservative investors this suggests that EM exposure needs to be modest by necessity. It is hard to have a big position in a volatile asset class when you're trying to keep the overall portfolio risk down.

Still, most portfolios, even more conservative ones, would benefit from having some EM exposure. While these countries and their securities are volatile, over the long term investors have been rewarded for accepting some volatility. During the past 27 years, an index of emerging market equities has outperformed a broad index of developed markets, including the United States, Europe and Japan (see Chart 2.9).

Chart 2.9: Emerging vs developed equity markets, 1990–2017

Source: Bloomberg, April 2017.

I return to the topic of sizing in the last chapter, but suffice to say that even a conservative portfolio, defined here as one with about a 40% allocation to stocks, could still stand to have 5%–7% in emerging market equities and perhaps another 2%–3% in dollar-denominated EM bonds. While these allocations will create more volatility in the short run, historically they have actually helped produce a more efficient portfolio.

Defining goals and limiting constraints

Building a portfolio starts with a goal. Broadly speaking that goal is normally total return or income. The next step is to decide how much risk the investor is willing to take. Next comes the issue of constraints, being limitations on the investment opportunity set. These are the assets the investor is either unwilling to own or ones they have decided to limit to a fixed amount. As a general rule, an investor should try to limit such constraints.

To be clear, no single constraint or exclusion will derail a portfolio. That said, there is a cumulative cost to having too many constraints. Sometimes the cost will be felt in lower returns. For example, investors who have ignored emerging markets have missed out on some impressive gains. More often, the loss will be felt in a less well-balanced portfolio. In other words, a portfolio that has a bit more risk than is necessary.

As will become clear in the subsequent chapters, the goal of an asset allocator is to arrive at an allocation that can deliver the highest expected return for a given level of risk. For those who believe they have the skill, returns can be enhanced through market timing, i.e. changing the allocation based on a perception of economic conditions, value and other market-driving considerations.

For others, the sensible course will be to arrive at a long-term allocation that is broadly consistent with risk objectives and stick to it. But for either the long-term strategic allocator or the market timer, the investor's job will be made easier if they have a broader set of markets at their disposal. Each limit or constraint creates a slightly less interesting opportunity set.

Key concepts

- ➥ The first step in portfolio construction is stating an objective. The objective can be total return, income or some combination of both. Regardless of the exact objective, the investor should be as explicit as possible. The objective will define the broad contours of the portfolio.

- ➥ Investors impose all sorts of constraints on portfolios, including geography, asset class or risk. While constraints are often necessary, they can also incur a cost: a less risk-efficient portfolio. The investor should try to loosen constraints wherever possible.

- ➥ One of the more damaging constraints is the home country bias, a tendency to invest exclusively or mostly in the investor's home country. This constraint is likely to harm investors, particularly those living in countries where financial markets are dominated by a relatively small number of companies or industries.

3

The Cost of a Good Night's Sleep: Considering Risk

M UCH OF THE previous chapter focused on constraints. The most important constraint for most investors is risk. While everyone wants more return, few investors are indifferent to risk. Given the primacy of risk in the investment process, this chapter will be exclusively dedicated to that topic. The goal will be to define risk and explore how risk constraints, otherwise known as the risk budget, will shape a portfolio. The key takeaway from this chapter is that an investor's willingness, or lack thereof, to tolerate risk will shape a portfolio more than any other factor.

Many investors insist that they have a high risk tolerance, but almost all studies suggest that people have a tendency to overstate their willingness to endure market volatility and losses. Too often behavioral biases work against investors, resulting in too many buying high and selling low.

Further complicating the process, risk is a slippery characteristic. While well defined in academic literature, the formal definition of risk does not easily translate into personal experience. When most investors think about risk they describe it in visceral terms, such as: How much can I lose?

Bridging the gap between the visceral and more formal definition of risk is key for portfolio construction. In building a portfolio, you need to go beyond the simple desire to avoid losses. Instead, the focus needs to be on how to measure, manage and minimize portfolio-level risk.

The risk budget

As we saw in the previous chapter, limiting asset classes or geographies can have a significant impact, often for the worse, on a portfolio. That said, there is a more significant and common constraint, and one that should in most cases be respected: risk. The price of being in the market is accepting some risk.

All portfolios contain some risk. Even a portfolio 100% invested in government bonds will fluctuate with changes in interest rates. An investor will receive the full value of the bonds at maturity, but on a day-to-day or even year-to-year basis, the value of the portfolio will change. And as investors move from safe government bonds to corporate bonds and further up the risk ladder, it gets more complicated.

Arriving at how much an investor is willing to see their portfolio move, and at times lose, is critical to arriving at the right asset allocation. The risk an investor is willing to tolerate will in large part define their long-term allocation. This is the concept behind the *risk budget*.

To understand why risk plays such a central role in building portfolios, it is first necessary to define the measure. The measure of risk most commonly used in academia, and the one that has subsequently been adopted by the financial industry, is not the one that pops into most investors' minds.

Ask most investors how they define risk and the most likely answer is how much money they might lose, or perhaps the probability of that loss. There is nothing wrong with either definition. Both are intuitive and as far as they go correct. The problem is they're just hard to plug into a system for building portfolios and for that reason a different definition is needed.

Defining risk

In this book, I adopt the more formal definitions of risk: the variance or standard deviation of returns, and in a few instances *beta*. These measures, particularly the standard deviation of returns, have several useful properties. The most important of these is that it allows for a simple and meaningful ratio: expected return versus expected risk. If nothing else, framing risk in this way allows investors to quickly and easily compare the relative attractiveness of different investments.

This is not to suggest that everyone agrees on this definition. Some find it too complicated. Others find it too simple and prefer more esoteric measures of risk. One measure focuses on downside risk, a measure known as semi-variance. There are other, even more complicated measures, such as value-at-risk (VAR), which is often employed by big banks. VAR focuses on the potential dollar amount a bank or other institution may lose within a specified time frame.

These measures all have their benefits, and in some circumstances provide a better measure of risk than the standard deviation of returns. The reason to focus on the latter is not that it is perfect, but that it is a relatively easy way to describe the risk of both a single security and an entire portfolio. It also has the added benefit of easily fitting into a formula to build portfolios, known as *mean variance optimization*, which I cover in Chapter 7.

Curves and tails

The concept of standard deviation is not specific to finance. It sits within a broader toolkit of statistical measures popular in just about every social science, including finance and economics.

The standard deviation quantifies the variation or dispersion in a set of numbers. The higher the standard deviation, the greater the dispersion. This measure is one of several that are basic to statistics. This is why the standard deviation is often referred to as the *second moment* of the distribution, with the first moment being the mean or average. Each moment helps describe the manner in which a set of numbers is distributed. To better understand the significance of the standard deviation, it is worth comparing it with the other moments.

The most basic statistical measure is the average or mean. The mean, or more formally the arithmetic mean, is calculated by taking all the observations and dividing the sum by the number of observations. The mean is sometimes referred to as a measure of central tendency. There are other measures of central tendency, including the medium, mode or trimmed-mean. What they have in common is that they are all constructed to describe what happens most of the time.

The mean can be thought of as the single number that best summarizes the data set. The standard deviation measures something else. If the mean is intended to provide a rough approximation of the most likely outcome, the standard deviation provides an indication of the relative *range* of outcomes. The higher the standard deviation, the more the outcome is likely to vary. If viewed from the perspective of the familiar bell curve, the higher the standard deviation, the more likely the unlikely. In other words, a higher standard deviation equates with more extreme occurrences (see Chart 3.1).

Chart 3.1: The normal distribution

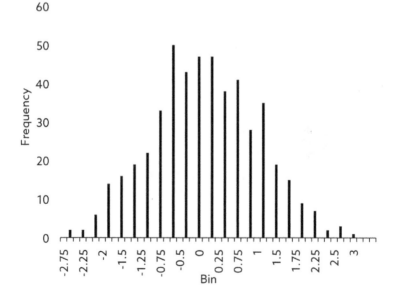

There are other *higher moments* of the distribution as well. The third moment is skew, which refers to the symmetry of the distribution. Distributions with positive or negative skew are not perfectly symmetrical like the bell curve in Chart 3.1. While not critical to portfolio construction, skew does come up in finance, particularly in options markets.

The fourth moment is a bit more abstract. It is known by the vaguely unhealthy sounding name of kurtosis. It refers to the extent to which there are more or fewer observations in the ends, or *tails*, of the distribution. Occasionally, more quantitative investment managers will refer to a fat tail outcome, which is a way of saying that something unexpected happened. Where fat tail outcomes occur, this means we are looking at a distribution with higher kurtosis.

In asset allocation, investors need to primarily rely on the mean, often referred to as the expected return, and the standard deviation. Sometimes variance is used instead of standard deviation, which is simply the square of the standard deviation. Both the mean and the standard deviation are typically expressed as annualized numbers.

Risk and expected return

Further tying the concept to practice, standard deviation helps an investor think about the range of potential outcomes. These can range from the very likely, to the sort of likely, to *this will never, ever happen*. This latter does occur with some degree of regularity in investing.

Consider this example of degrees of likelihood for stocks. To simplify the numbers a bit, in the United States the long-term total return of stocks has been somewhere in the vicinity of 10%, while the annualized risk, measured by the standard deviation, has been approximately 15%. We can use these estimates to calculate the approximate likelihood of various returns.

To the extent stock market returns follow what is known as the normal distribution, about two-thirds of the observations will be between +1 and -1 standard deviations from the mean. In the above example this translates into roughly a 65% probability that stock returns will be between 25% and -5% in a given year. To arrive at this you simply add and subtract the standard deviation to the expected mean (10% + 15% = 25% and 10% - 15% = -5%).

What about less likely occurrences? In theory a range of two standard deviations should contain about 95% of all occurrences. This means that 95% of the time the market will return between 40% and -20%, the equivalent of 2 standard deviations above and below the mean (10% + (2*15%) = 40% and 10% - (2*15%) = -20%). By using the standard deviation you can approximate a rough range of returns for any asset class.

Fat tails and the impossible

The problem of course is that unlike physics, in which reality conforms to mathematics, the social sciences are messier. There is no physical law of nature that decrees that stock returns follow a normal distribution. In fact, they don't. The normal distribution is simply a reasonable approximation, with at least one important caveat: in finance the tails are fat. One of the dirty little secrets of financial theory is that really unlikely events, or fat tail events, occur much more frequently than financial theory suggests they should.

One good example of this is the 1987 stock market crash, when the S&P 500 dropped more than 20% in a single day. Based on a long-term measure of market volatility, this should simply never have happened. If markets really followed a normal distribution, the type of volatility spike represented below (see Chart 3.2) *might* occasionally occur, every billion years or so.

The reason we get crashes more often than theory predicts, or we would like, is that markets are always changing; human interactions are not as neat or predictable as in the physical world. This is one reason why economists are often accused of *physics envy*.

If financial reality conformed to financial theory, crashes like 1987 or the more recent flash crash of 2010, when the Dow Jones Industrial Average plunged and then subsequently rebounded 1,000 points within minutes, would be unheard of. Instead, while the normal distribution is a useful tool, it is an admittedly imperfect one. Unlike theory, bad stuff happens with an alarming degree of frequency.

Chart 3.2: S&P 500 10-Day realized volatility, February 1986 to December 1988

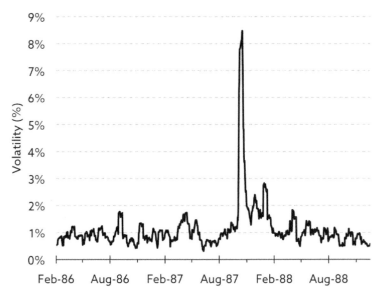

Source: Bloomberg, March 2017.

Still a useful model

While the normal distribution is not a wholly accurate model of financial markets, nor standard deviation the perfect measure of risk, they are both important tools that should not be easily discarded. Unlikely events do occur with a disturbing regularity, but these limitations do not invalidate the practical benefits of using standard deviation as a measure of risk.

One of those practical benefits is that while unlikely events happen, most of the time risk is a fairly stable concept. In fact, you can be more confident of a risk forecast than you can be of a return forecast. The historical volatility of different asset classes is in fact a useful predictor of future volatility. This makes historical volatility a key input for portfolio construction, and we turn to this in the next section.

Key concepts: nature of risk

→ Risk can be measured in different ways. While there is no single correct definition, variance or standard deviation is typically used in portfolio construction.

→ The standard deviation of returns is a measure of the dispersion of outcomes. The greater the standard deviation, the more likely you will observe outcomes that differ substantially from the average.

→ While easy to work with, standard deviation has one big drawback: significant market dislocations occur much more frequently than theory suggests.

→ That said, historical volatility provides a reasonable proxy for future volatility, making it an important input in portfolio construction.

Setting a risk budget

Having established a definition of risk, the next step is to think about how risk is factored into a portfolio's asset allocation. While obviously not the only determinant, the risk level an investor targets will guide the broad allocations to the different asset classes. Roughly speaking, a low risk budget means more bonds and cash, and less stocks. A high risk target translates into more stocks, high-yield bonds and other risky assets.

This leads to a different question, which is how to determine the appropriate risk budget for an investor. How people should assess their appetite for risk is tricky and in many ways it is better suited to psychology than finance. Surveys and questionnaires try to get at this by asking how an investor would react to different market events. It is not clear that people's answers in such surveys always conform to their behavior. This is one reason why many advisors and financial professionals fall back on an old tool: asking the investor, "When do you need the money?"

The longer the time horizon, the more risk the investor should be willing to bear. This is why young workers who are starting to invest for retirement should have the riskiest portfolios. They won't need the money for many decades and they are best positioned to withstand the volatility of stocks and other risky assets. As individuals approach retirement, the portfolio should shift into less risky investments to ensure that the money is there when they need it.

Given this dynamic between age and risk tolerance, many advisors advocate an allocation based on age. Using this approach, the target allocation for a 30-year-old would be more aggressive, with a much higher allocation to stocks, than the target allocation for a 60-year-old. While imperfect, age or time to retirement can provide a reasonable, first approximation of how much risk an investor can take.

While age makes for a reasonable starting point, investors should incorporate at least two other considerations: personality and personal circumstances. Starting with the former, to state the incredibly obvious, different investors have different personalities. Nobody follows the exact risk profile dictated by their age or years to retirement.

Some people are genuinely more risk seeking, while others are more conservative. Part of the role of a financial advisor is to help clients come to some realistic assessment of where they fall on the spectrum. As a general rule, be realistic. The best way to think about risk is to consider how much pain the investor is willing to bear.

That next consideration – personal circumstances – involves whether or not the investor can afford to be conservative. Investors that are under-saved may need to consider a riskier portfolio to generate a sufficient stream of income to support their retirement. As discussed in the introduction, longer lifespans and low rates have conspired to complicate retirement funding. Conversely, more affluent investors that have over-saved may practically decide that they can afford to take less risk.

Finally, when trying to map someone's tolerance for risk to an actual portfolio, another useful trick is to go back to our definition of risk, the standard deviation. For example, let's assume a more conservative stock/bond portfolio will produce an annual return of 5% a year with an 8% standard deviation. This would suggest about a 5% chance that the portfolio might lose more than 10% in a single year. If we further assume that the standard deviation has a tendency to underestimate extreme conditions, the actual probability of a loss of that magnitude is probably greater, say a 10% chance of losing 10% in a single year.

If an investor never wants to experience a drawdown of that magnitude, a portfolio with a target risk of 8%, measured by the standard deviation of returns, is probably too much. That investor should look for a more conservative portfolio, probably one with more bonds and cash. If on the other hand the investor turns up their nose at a 5% return, more risk is in order. Risk helps define the type of portfolio the investor should own. In both examples – conservative and aggressive – risk also determines what proportion of a portfolio should be held in stocks.

Equities, the big driver of risk

An investor's portfolio risk will largely be driven by the percentage allocation to equities. When you line up various stock/bond allocations, sometimes referred to as model portfolios, you'll see that the allocation to stocks vs bonds explains the vast majority of the change in risk.

Chart 3.3 illustrates this point. Four portfolios are comprised of two simple building blocks: an exchange traded fund (ETF) representing the S&P 500 and an ETF representing the Barclays US Aggregate Bond Index. The only difference between the four portfolios is the percentage allocated to stocks vs bonds.

The first portfolio is comprised of 20% stocks and 80% bonds. Each of the remaining three portfolios add 20% to the stock portion and subtract 20% from the bond portion, with the final portfolio comprised of 80% stocks and 20% bonds. As the percentage allocated to stocks rises, the risk of the overall portfolio also rises. Remember, nothing else changes in the portfolio. The types of stocks or bonds is not altered – simply the allocation to each of the two asset classes.

Chart 3.3: Stock/bond allocation and portfolio risk

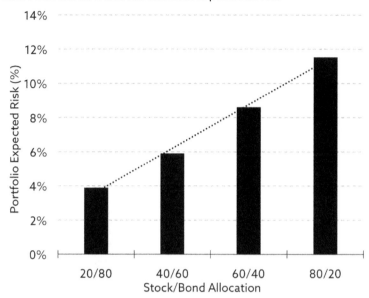

Source: BlackRock Aladdin Portfolio Builder, iShares, March 2017.

This illustrates a key concept. Regardless of what else is in a portfolio, much of the overall portfolio risk comes from the percentage allocated to equities. While the risk can be changed somewhat, depending on the type of stocks, the reality is that more stocks equate to more risk. This is a simple function of stocks being much more volatile than bonds or cash.

To further illustrate the point it is worth diving deeper into the sources of risk. Let's consider a 40/60 stock/bond portfolio – with 40% invested in stocks and 60% in bonds. For simplicity's sake, in this example I use an all-US portfolio. The stock portion is invested entirely in the S&P 500. The remaining portion is invested in the Barclays Aggregate Index, which is comprised of US government bonds, mortgage-backed securities and some investment grade corporate bonds. This portfolio is very conservative; probably too conservative for most. The expected risk is a little under 6% annualized.

Now look one level deeper. The risk can be further decomposed to see where most of it comes from. The first thing to notice is that the interest rate risk is a very small portion of the overall risk (see Chart 3.4). Fluctuations in rates should have only a modest impact on the overall portfolio's return.

Chart 3.4: Risk factor decomposition in a US 40/60 portfolio

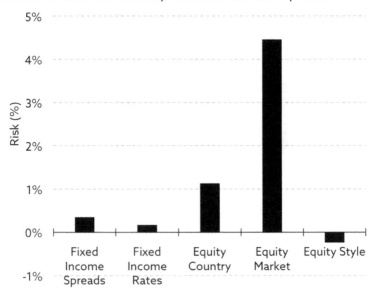

Source: BlackRock Aladdin Portfolio Builder, iShares March 2017.

This seems like a bit of an odd result. The portfolio is after all 60% bonds. More importantly, the constituents of the Barclays Index are mostly traditional bonds, whose price is heavily influenced by changes in rates. Shouldn't rates be a bigger contributor to overall risk?

The reason rates don't affect things more is that while most of the portfolio is made up of bonds, remember that bond volatility is a fraction of equity volatility. Even if rates move a great deal, the impact on the bond portion is modest relative to the volatility that the equity portion can and frequently does experience.

What does drive the portfolio is equity risk. To be even more specific, the big contributor is the risk associated with the overall equity market, which makes up around 4.5% of the 6% in total risk. A more modest portion is the risk that is specific to the *US equity market*, as opposed to say European stocks.

This means that between the risk associated with equity markets in general and the risk specific to the US equity market, equity risk accounts for approximately 90% of the overall risk of the portfolio. This is an important concept. The sample portfolio is mostly bonds. The stocks the portfolio does hold are relatively stable, large US companies. The reader will notice that there are no international stocks, no emerging market stocks. Yet, even with these US stocks as a minority of the overall allocation, equities still account for the overwhelming majority of the portfolio's risk.

The hierarchy of risks

That stocks will generally account for most of the risk in the portfolio is a safe bet. While volatility can and does shift, it would be rare for bond volatility to surpass stock volatility or for gold to suddenly be less volatile than investment grade bonds. This makes our definition of risk – historic volatility measured by standard deviation – useful in that it can be relied on as a reasonable proxy for the future volatility of the major asset classes.

While stocks normally produce higher returns than bonds or cash, there are plenty of years when the reverse happens and bonds beat stocks. However, there are no instances when the standard deviation of cash, assuming no foreign exchange risk, was higher than the standard deviation of bonds. It is also highly unlikely that bonds have a year when they're riskier than stocks.

Looking at the past 40 years of data bears out the notion that bond market volatility is almost always lower than equity market volatility. This is even true during those periods when bonds are experiencing losses.

Chart 3.5 tracks the standard deviation of US stock and bond returns. The measure is calculated using the trailing 60 months of return data. Note that even in periods when bonds have been unusually volatile, such as the early 1980s, bond market volatility has still been considerably lower than equity market volatility.

Chart 3.5: Volatility of stocks and bonds

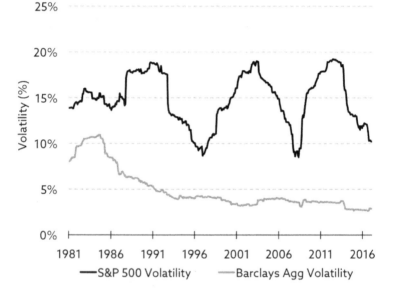

Source: Bloomberg, April 2017.

The stability of the relationship reflects the fact that stocks are rarely spared bond market volatility. If bonds are getting hit, stocks are probably getting hit worse. Other than a recession, there are few better ways to scare stock investors than watching their more staid cousins in the bond market panic. When bonds sell-off, stock investors not only follow, but normally sell with even greater abandon.

As of mid-2017, markets were actually in the opposite state. Unusually calm bond markets were having a soothing effect on stock investors, with both stock and bond market volatility near all-time lows. This state of affairs, which has persisted now for many years, is arguably a function of unprecedented monetary accommodation by central banks. When and if bond market volatility finally picks up, it is a safe bet that stock market volatility will follow.

Does low for longer = lower risk?

When interest rates are exceptionally low, as they have been for many years, investors are forced into riskier assets in order to generate a reasonable return. In other words, regardless of an investor's view on an asset class, they are inclined to buy riskier assets given a lack of alternatives. If hiding out in cash produces no real return, and long-term bonds little better, investors gravitate to riskier securities, such as high-yield or emerging market bonds, out of desperation. This creates a tendency to *buy the dips* or *stretch for yield*, which has the effect of suppressing volatility.

That said, the effect can also go into reverse. When monetary accommodation is withdrawn or rates unexpectedly rise, as they did in the spring of 2013, volatility comes back with a vengeance.

This should be a concern for investors. While central banks in Europe and Japan are still buying billions of dollars of bonds every month, the Fed is in the process of raising rates. By late 2017 they are likely to begin allowing their bloated balance sheet to shrink, which will entail no longer reinvesting the proceeds from maturing securities. All of which means that in the coming years monetary policy will be less accommodative than it has been in the ten years to 2017.

When monetary and financial market conditions are less lax, volatility is more likely to rise. This suggests that today's low volatility environment is unlikely to last, which in turn suggests the absolute level of volatility for both stocks and bonds may be a good deal higher in the future.

Intra-asset class: nuances in risk

Let's return to the relationship between asset classes and volatility. While stocks are more volatile than bonds, there are differences between stocks.

For that matter, there are also differences between conservative Treasury bonds and more speculative high-yield or emerging market bonds.

As such, it is worth considering some nuances to the general rules described above. While the first driver of risk in a portfolio is the broad allocation to stocks versus bonds, the *types* of stocks and bonds will also have a material impact on overall portfolio risk.

To start, investors should certainly be cognizant of the differences in volatility between US and international stocks. US stocks have historically been less volatile than international stocks. Part of this is a function of the composition of the US market, which is heavily weighted towards higher-quality companies, i.e. companies with reliable earnings streams. It is also, from the perspective of a US investor, a function of currency exposure. When a US-based investor invests in an international market she is exposed to not only the fluctuation of the underlying asset, but also the currency in which that asset is denominated. As the currency will rise and fall, in addition to movements in the underlying stock or bond, this introduces another source of volatility. Clearly, this second point about currency exposure also applies equally to investors in other countries – UK, Japan, Germany, etc. – when they invest outside their domestic equity market.

Apart from the risk associated with a foreign currency, there are important differences between various segments of the domestic equity market. Even for investors who have adopted a complete home country bias, the choice of stocks or funds can have a significant impact on the overall portfolio risk.

Take a very stylized example: two portfolios, the first consisting of bank and technology companies, and the second consisting of healthcare companies and food and beverage firms. The first set, banks and technology, are generally more volatile than the broader market. This is particularly true for smaller, less established technology firms and mid-sized banks.

In contrast, utility companies and food and beverage firms tend to be some of the least volatile companies. Both industries are characterized by relatively reliable business models and earnings streams. In investment terms, they are less cyclical than other types of businesses. Thus the volatility of these sectors tends to be more modest than the overall stock market.

Beta

To illustrate the tendency for certain sectors to be riskier than others it is helpful to introduce a somewhat different notion of risk: *beta*. The topic of beta is covered more completely in Chapter 5, but it is useful to introduce the concept in this context.

At a basic level, stocks and sectors that tend to be more volatile than the broader market have a beta greater than 1. At the opposite end of the spectrum, lower risk utility and food companies are likely to have a beta below 1, suggesting that they go up less than the market on up days and fall less on down days.

Translating a beta into returns is relatively simple. Roughly speaking, a stock or sector with a beta of 1.2 would be expected to advance roughly 1.2% on average if the broader market was up 1%. A stock or sector with a beta of 0.8 would be expected to gain less than the broader market, approximately 0.8%. Beta is another way to view volatility, not in absolute terms but relative to the broader market.

Looking at the betas of various market segments illustrates the concept of varying levels of risk. Certain sectors consistently have a beta below 1. Industries and sectors that are more cyclical, and therefore experience more volatility in their earnings, can be relied on to generally have a beta above 1 (see Chart 3.6).

The lesson is that an investor could have a portfolio of stocks made up of mostly low beta companies and sectors, often referred to as *defensives*. At the opposite end of the spectrum an investor could build a portfolio comprised of more volatile and speculative high beta companies.

In either instance stocks will still be the big contributor to portfolio risk. However, *how much* incremental risk they generate will partly be determined by any biases in the portfolio. An equity portion comprised of low beta, low volatility companies can generally be relied on to be calmer than a high beta portfolio.

Chart 3.6: US sector betas

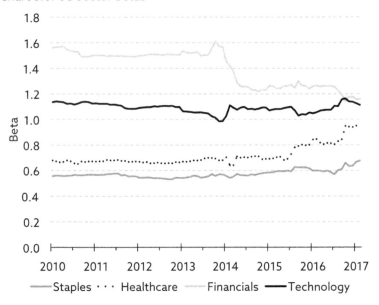

Source: Bloomberg, March 2017.

This is important as the relationship between beta and risk will impact the overall risk of a portfolio. The higher the beta, the greater the risk contribution from your equity holdings. For portfolios that are invested primarily in broad-based mutual funds, this is not much of an issue. Unless an investor goes out of their way to emphasize higher risk segments of the market, the average fund beta should approximate the market.

However, for investors who prefer to focus on specific, higher beta areas of the market, say high-tech or small companies, the volatility of the equity portfolio is likely to be higher than the broader stock market. This means that unless risk is offset in other parts of the portfolio, for example by buying more low-risk bonds, the overall portfolio risk will be higher.

Asset class cross-dressing

Just as some stocks can be more or less volatile than the broader market, some bonds can also deviate from the traditional characteristics of their asset class. High-yield bonds, for example, have volatility that under certain circumstances, i.e. severe market corrections, can approach that of equities.

And as previously demonstrated, not all stocks are as volatile as the market. Not only are some equities lower beta, but there are certain types of stocks, notably utility companies, that often trade more in line with interest rates than the stock market. All of which suggests that investors should be aware of those exceptions when stocks act like bonds and bonds act like stocks.

High-yield bonds provide a good example of this phenomenon. Returning to our previous example of the 40/60 stock/bond portfolio, what if our theoretical investor decided their objective was income rather than total return? In today's yield-starved environment, traditional bonds don't pay much. One way to lift the income would be to own riskier bonds, such as high-yield bonds, that typically pay a higher interest rate compared to traditional government bonds.

The 40/60 portfolio in the original example would yield around 2.25%. Now assume half the bond allocation is shifted to an index fund dedicated to high-yield bonds. The overall portfolio has the same 60% allocated to bonds. However, half of those bonds will now be in riskier, high-yield instruments. Accordingly, the portfolio will behave somewhat differently.

On the plus side, the inclusion of high-yield bonds substantially improves the amount of income the portfolio produces. The trailing 12-month yield rises from roughly 2.25% to around 3.10%, a substantial pickup in a low-yield world.

The downside: this is not a free lunch. By substituting 30% of the portfolio with a riskier asset class, the risk composition is drastically changed. While the original 40/60 example had a risk of slightly under 6%, the new portfolio has a risk of around 7%. The investor has bought him or herself around 0.90% more of income each year. The cost of doing so is an almost identical increase, around 90 bps, in risk.

So far this makes sense. You buy riskier bonds and get more income at the cost of marginally more risk. What is surprising is the source of the extra risk. It does not all come from where you'd expect. It primarily comes from two areas: credit spreads and equities.

The spread component represents the difference between the yield on the high-yield bonds and a comparable Treasury instrument. When the spread is narrow, investors are willing to accept a smaller premium in incremental yield. When the spread widens, investors are demanding a bigger premium, indicating more compensation is needed to bear the risk of a default. The incremental risk associated with high-yield is measured relative to that spread.

That part is intuitive. You add high-yield and you get more credit-related risk. What is less intuitive is the contribution to risk from equities. How does buying a bond, even a riskier bond, result in incrementally more equity risk?

While high-yield bonds entail more risk of default than other bonds, they are still bonds. They have covenants, i.e. legal protections, granting bond holders certain rights, they mature on a specified date and they generally pay investors a fixed-rate of annual interest. Yet, despite clearly being bonds, adding high-yield to the portfolio also adds to equity risk, even though the allocation to equities remain constant.

High-yield bonds add around 0.30% of annual equity-related risk to the portfolio (see Chart 3.7). The reason high-yield adds equity risk is that while high-yield bonds are technically bonds, in practice they often behave more like stocks.

High-yield, along with emerging market debt, is one of the riskier segments of the bond market. When investors are cautious they typically shun high-yield. When investors are more optimistic they are more willing to accept the incremental risk inherent in the asset class. As a result, high-yield bonds often move more in-line with equities, another risky asset class, rather than other types of bonds.

This relationship can be seen by looking at the correlation between high-yield and equities. Recall in Chapter 1 that over the long term, US equities and traditional US bonds had a zero correlation. More recently, Treasuries and US large cap stocks have had a reliably negative correlation. Now compare that relationship with the one between US large cap stocks and US high-yield bonds, measured by the returns on the S&P 500 and Barclays High Yield Index respectively.

Chart 3.7: Risk factor decomposition for a US 40/60 portfolio with high-yield bonds

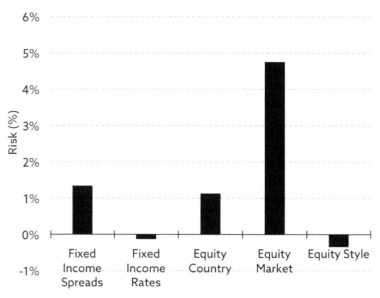

Source: BlackRock Aladdin Portfolio Builder, iShares, March 2017.

As with the previous stock-bond correlation, this measure moves around over time. During the past 20 years, the correlation has been as low as 0.1, indicating a statistically insignificant relationship, and as high as 0.80. In more recent years, the correlation has been relatively steady at 0.60 (see Chart 3.8). But while the correlation fluctuates, unlike the correlation between stocks and Treasuries it is always *positive*. Stocks and high-yield tend to move together to a statistically significant degree.

Chart 3.8: US equity – high-yield correlations

Source: Bloomberg, March 2017.

The strong correlation between stocks and high-yield bonds is the cause of high-yield's contribution to equity risk. To the extent stocks and high-yield tend to move together, high-yield can be thought of as adding risk that is indistinguishable from that of stocks. As a result, adding high-yield actually adds to equity risk.

This brings up an important point to be covered in the next chapter. Regardless of the asset class, always ask yourself whether an investment is diversifying the major risks already embedded in a portfolio. In the case of high-yield, this actually adds to the biggest risk, i.e. equity risk. There are periods in the market cycle when an investor would arguably be happy to add to equity risk through incremental high-yield exposure. The point is to be aware that this is what is happening.

The Jessica Seinfeld approach: sneaking in exposures

Many years ago Jessica Seinfeld, wife of comedian Jerry Seinfeld, wrote a bestselling cookbook. The premise was simple: you can sneak healthy foods past finicky children, and occasionally finicky spouses, by blending them up and adding them to most dishes. Children won't be inclined to spit out their broccoli if it is hidden in their brownies.

Sneaking in exposures can also be put to work in portfolio construction. The plus side of the occasionally blurry line between asset classes is that the investor can get creative. For example, low-beta, dividend-paying stocks can add to yield and dampen down volatility, while still providing equity exposure.

Today, many investors have reasonably decided that rather than relying on low-yielding bonds for income and downside protection, it is better to allocate a certain percentage of their fixed-income allocation to a low-beta equity fund. This approach allows investors to maintain some downside protection, while adding yield into a different part of their portfolio.

Alternatively, an investor worried about market volatility, but not a bear market, could substitute high-yield bonds for a portion of their equity allocation. This would lower beta while increasing yield. A similar argument could be made with other, hybrid asset classes, such as preferred stock, which has characteristics of both stocks and bonds.

In both cases, the opportunity is to use an asset class in a non-traditional way. Bonds are not the only source of income. In some cases, low-beta, dividend-paying stocks may be a more efficient source of yield. At the same time, if you expect a flat stock market, high-yield can be thought of as a higher-yielding equity substitute. Sometimes, the best way to build a portfolio is to make more use of stock-like-bonds and bond-like-stocks.

Adding by subtraction

To conclude the chapter it is worth examining the question of how to lower overall portfolio risk. If risk is primarily a function of equity exposure, and if even certain bonds can add to equity risk, what are some ways to lower it? What asset classes are best positioned to mitigate the big source of risk – equities – in most portfolios?

Chart 3.9: Gold one-year realized volatility (%)

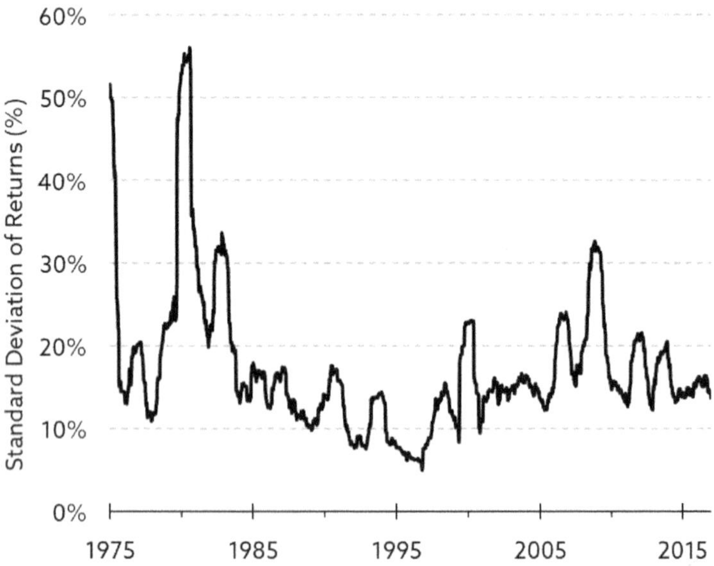

Source: Bloomberg, April 2017.

The answer is to find an asset class with a zero or negative correlation to stocks. As highlighted in Chapter 1, bonds have played this role in recent years. While this cannot be taken for granted, absent a more aggressive central bank, traditional government bonds are likely to continue to play that role, albeit maybe not quite as effectively.

The other obvious way to mitigate risk is cash. As some family members will quip when you don't know what to buy them as a gift, cash always works. While cash and cash substitutes don't provide much in the way of yield, the addition of cash will dampen overall portfolio-level volatility.

A third, and far less obvious example, is gold. Gold is less obvious because, unlike traditional bonds and cash, it is a particularly volatile asset class. It is true that gold is volatile; often more volatile than stocks. Looking back over the past 35 years, the average volatility – measured as the one-year standard deviation of weekly returns – has been approximately 17% (see Chart 3.9).

Despite its volatility, gold can actually mitigate overall portfolio volatility. As demonstrated in the previous chapter, gold's value is its propensity to rise, or at least fall less, during periods of volatility. It is worth considering the impact of that characteristic at the portfolio level. The argument in favor of gold is that it is uncorrelated with paper assets, such as stocks and bonds. The fact is an asset can be volatile, even very volatile, and still help lower risk to the extent it is negatively correlated with most of your other assets.

To illustrate the impact on the overall portfolio, let's return to the classic 60/40 portfolio of US stocks and bonds (60% stocks and 40% bonds). As of the spring of 2017, that portfolio would have a risk of approximately 8.60%. Now consider what happens when you shift the allocation by lowering the equity exposure by 10%, and adding a 10% allocation to gold.

At first glance you'd expect the overall portfolio risk to rise given gold's volatility. Instead, the risk actually drops by around 1%, to 7.60%

The reason risk drops is that gold generally provides risk mitigation when most needed: periods of financial stress. This can be seen by examining the performance of the two portfolios – with and without gold – during two periods of unusual volatility. During both the 2008 financial crisis and the market sell-off surrounding the 2011 downgrade of US debt, the portfolio with gold (50/40/10) suffered a smaller loss than the traditional (60/40) portfolio (see Chart 3.10).

During the financial crisis, when stocks and other risky assets were suffering through the worst bear market in decades, gold rose for much of the period. From mid-November of 2008 to February 2009, gold rose by nearly 40%.

We see a similar pattern around the period surrounding the downgrade of US debt in 2011. During those summer months, when there was massive uncertainty surrounding US debt, gold rose by over 25%.

Chart 3.10: Performance of two portfolios – 60/40 and 50/40/10 – during drawdowns (%)

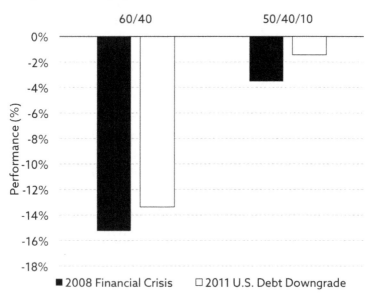

Source: BlackRock Aladdin Portfolio Builder, April 2017.

In the spirit of full disclosure, in the above examples gold did not do so well once the panic ended. Following both periods, gold sank as investors rotated back into stocks, high-yield bonds and other risky assets.

In addition, gold does not always work. Depending on the source of the volatility gold may add to risk. This was certainly the case in early 2013 when stocks, bonds *and* gold all sank together. Gold in particular got hit, down around 20%, as investors fretted over US monetary policy. In that instance the Fed did not even need to raise rates to tank gold, they just needed to muse about the possibility.

Still, in most other instances gold managed to provide diversification when most other markets were falling. This is a good illustration of why even a volatile asset can be helpful, assuming it is sufficiently uncorrelated with everything else in your portfolio.

Key concepts: sources of risk

➤ Equities are generally the greatest source of risk in a portfolio. As a result, risk will generally increase in proportion to the percentage of stocks.

➤ While equities are riskier than bonds, there are nuances within each asset class. Stocks with more stable business models and less cyclicality tend to be less risky than the broader market.

➤ Not all bonds are low risk. In particular, high-yield bonds can often behave more like stocks.

➤ To mitigate portfolio-level risk, add low-risk assets like traditional bonds or assets that are negatively correlated with the rest of the portfolio.

4

Not Dead Yet: Why Diversification Still Matters

THE GOAL OF portfolio construction is to build an efficient portfolio, with efficiency defined as the maximum return per unit of risk. In some cases this takes the form of maximizing return for a given risk target. Another approach is to start with a return target and attempt to minimize risk. Either way, the goal is to maximize return for the risk you're willing to take. In order to better deliver on that objective, investors need to embrace diversification. Unfortunately, this has not been a particularly popular concept of late.

Buying American and getting into bad habits

Earlier, I discussed the market euphoria of the late 1990s. In retrospect, investor optimism at that moment appears silly, but it didn't seem so irrational at the time. Today, investors can also be forgiven for thinking all one needs to do is buy an index fund of US companies and settle in for consistent double digit returns.

The bull market that has followed the financial crisis has been a profitable time for investors. By mid-2017, stocks had more than tripled since the 2009 lows.

At the same time, and despite the rush into risky assets, traditional bonds have also done well. This comes as a shock, and disappointment, to those who forecasted that lax central bank policies would eventually lead to inflation and a bond market meltdown. While bond returns have not equaled the stellar performance of the 1980s, for a low-rate environment bonds have been a remarkably steady performer.

The unexpected but steady performance of bonds has also added to the sense of complacency. Despite dire predictions of surging interest rates, yields have remained low and bonds have done surprisingly well. In the seven years from 2009 to 2016, the Barclays Aggregate Index (AGG) of bonds has produced annualized returns of around 3.6%. Not only have returns been unexpectedly strong, they have also been surprisingly steady. In the seven years following the end of the financial crisis, there was only one year in which the total return to the AGG was negative.

This combination of a strong stock market and steady bond market has resulted in a sort of nirvana for investors, or at least US ones. As the two basic building blocks of most portfolios have done well at the same time, it has been possible to take a basic approach and produce stellar returns. Indeed, a simple 60/40 split of US stocks and bonds has been extremely hard to beat in this recent period – and for a generation now. Since 1990, a blended portfolio invested in 60% US stocks and 40% US bonds has produced annualized returns of roughly 9%.

And the results have only gotten better in recent years. Since 2009 the average annual return on that 60/40 US portfolio has been roughly 10.5%. These are attractive returns under any circumstances, particularly for a simple, domestically-oriented portfolio. The results become incredible, bordering on surreal, when you consider that the returns have been delivered with little volatility. For investors the takeaway is simple: on a risk-adjusted basis, this period has been about as good as it gets.

Given the success of the *keep-it-simple-stupid* approach, diversification has gotten a bad name. Why venture into more exotic assets when the simplest portfolio has performed the best? Those investors who have tried to build more diversified portfolios have underperformed simpler approaches since the financial crisis.

But, this is unlikely to continue.

Why simple may no longer suffice

The challenge going forward is that the very success of these two asset classes – US stocks and US bonds – contains the seeds of a less rosy future. For the first time in decades, both US stocks and bonds are expensive at the same time. This suggests lower returns over the next decade and probably a rougher, more volatile environment than investors have become accustomed to. In order to combat this headwind, investors need to consider casting a wider net. This means owning a more geographically diversified portfolio.

At this point many investors will object. They would rightly point out that many have been calling for a downturn in US assets for some time. Why should the good times not continue indefinitely, or at least for a few more years?

Low yields and stretched stocks

The simple answer is that US stocks and bonds are expensive. As discussed in more detail in Chapter 6, the fact that they're expensive tells you little about returns over the next month or quarter. However, stretched valuations tell you a great deal about what you can expect over the next three to five years. On that basis, those basic building blocks are looking less enticing.

Let's start with bonds.

Observing that bonds are expensive is the same thing as saying yields are low. This matters because the best predictor of long-term bond returns is simply the yield-to-maturity. In more simple terms, over the long term the return you generate on a bond will approximate the yield you are receiving.

At the time of writing, the yield-to-maturity on a US government bond is approximately 2.25%, while it is 1% in the United Kingdom and 0.50% in Germany. This suggests that investors should expect modest returns from bonds over the next ten years. The outlook obviously looks worse once you factor in inflation and the fact that most investors have to pay taxes on at least some of the interest.

And while it is true that rates have been low throughout the recovery from the financial crisis, and bonds have still produced decent returns, there is less room today to offset low rates with price appreciation. In order for prices to rise, which would add to the total return on bonds, yields need to decline from already low levels. This is particularly a problem for investors in Europe, where many intermediate maturity bonds still yield less than 1%.

Given current rates, in order to come close to a 3% or 4% return on the bond portion of a portfolio, investors will either need to consider other types of bonds, such as high-yield, or hope that rates fall even further from here. With central banks starting to moderate accommodation, another drop in rates is unlikely outside of an economic downturn.

And what about the other main asset, stocks?

If bonds return less can investors at least look forward to several more years of double digit stock returns? Is there a reason stocks cannot continue to rally?

Contrary to popular wisdom, bull markets do not die of old age. They need to be killed. The usual suspects are aggressive central banks and/or a recession. As of this writing, neither appears imminent.

That said, while bull markets do not die of old age and there is no physical law that prevents markets from marching higher, there is one factor that is likely to pull stocks, particularly US stocks, back to earth: valuations. To be sure, this is much more of an issue for US stocks than for the rest of the world. But as the United States comprises roughly 50% of the global stock market, it will be difficult for global stocks to shake off a severe US correction or bear market.

Paying up

While the US stock market still appears in decent health – profitable companies, low inflation and an accelerating economy – much of the good news has already been reflected in stock prices. With the bull market now the second longest in history, the market is much more richly priced than it was when stocks began to recover in 2009.

Since the bottom of the bear market, investors have been increasingly willing to pay higher and higher valuations for stocks. In early 2009, the bottom for global equities, investors were paying only 12x earnings for the S&P 500. By the first quarter of 2017 that multiple had risen to 22.

The rise in valuations illustrates an important caveat for investors too enamored with the US equity market. While the US has indeed led the global economic recovery, much of the rally in US stocks has not come from stronger earnings. In fact, 2015 and most of 2016 were distinguished by falling earnings. Instead, the bull market has been aided and abetted by higher multiples, i.e. investors willing to pay more for a dollar of earnings. This phenomenon is known as *multiple expansion* and it has dominated the US market in recent years (see Chart 4.1).

Chart 4.1: US equity valuations (trailing P/E of S&P 500)

Source: Bloomberg, April 2017.

An optimist might correctly point out that this phenomenon can continue, especially if interest rates stay low; low interest rates tend to support higher multiples. There is some truth to this. Market multiples tend to be higher when both nominal rates and inflation are low.

An optimist could also point out that multiple expansion can continue for some time. The current bout of US multiple expansion has been relatively modest, at least compared to what happened in the 1980s and 1990s. Why shouldn't the bull market celebrate its 10th or even 11th anniversary?

The first challenge is that the factors that drove consistent years of multiple expansion in the 1980s and 1990s are difficult to repeat. At the time investors were celebrating a secular decline in inflation and interest rates. Both inflation and interest rates dropped from the double digit levels of the 1970s and early 1980s to the low single digits of more recent years.

As rates dropped, multiples expanded. This is consistent with theory and somewhat intuitive. Basic finance theory tells you that if the rate used to discount future earnings goes down, prices should go up. Unfortunately, this is not a repeatable phenomenon.

While rates can theoretically move lower, as the experiences in continental Europe and Japan demonstrate, rates cannot decline as much as they already have. If they were to drop towards or below the lows witnessed in the summer of 2016, that would probably suggest a global recession, not an environment in which equities are likely to thrive.

The second difference between today and the early 1980s is price, or more specifically valuations. Multiples expanded in those decades because they were starting from a much lower base. Today, most valuation metrics are already elevated relative to history.

In fact, by a few measures companies in the United States have never been this expensive outside the tech bubble of the late 1990s. Chart 4.2 tracks the cyclically adjusted price-to-earnings ratio (CAPE). This valuation metric compares price to earnings over an economic cycle, traditionally measured as a decade. This is in contrast to a traditional P/E ratio that is based on a single year of earnings.

While there is nothing particularly significant about the CAPE, it is a useful measure of long-term value. By this measure, the US equity market has only previously been *this* expensive in the late 1990s.

Chart 4.2: Cyclically adjusted P/E ratio (CAPE) of US equities

Source: BlackRock, Bloomberg, April 2017.

Not only is there not much room for multiples to continue to grow from here, but even today's levels suggest caution. Just as the current yield on a bond is a reasonable proxy for long-term returns, the multiple on a stock or stock index tells you something about long-term future returns for equities. The relationship is not as reliable as a bond's yield, but valuations matter, particularly for longer time horizons.

As Chart 4.3 illustrates, high valuations (top quartile) typically produce much lower returns over the next one to three years than average or below-average valuations. Today's multiples suggest, at a minimum, much lower returns in the coming years.

Chart 4.3: Cyclically adjusted P/E ratio (CAPE) of US equities

	Average one-year return	Average three-year return
Bottom quartile valuation (cheapest)	11.53%	33.73%
Middle two quartiles valuation (average)	9.56%	33.25%
Top quartile valuation (most expensive)	4.09%	8.92%

Source: Bloomberg, March 2017.

The lesson, particularly for US investors or those with a bias towards US equity markets, is that while simple – a 60/40 stocks/bonds portfolio – has been spectacular since the financial crisis (and indeed since 1990), this effect is unlikely to continue.

The very forces that provided such stellar returns make a repeat performance unlikely. While valuations can and have gone higher for stocks, and yields have been lower for bonds, both are unlikely to happen at the same time. This suggests that either US stocks, bonds or both are likely to disappoint.

It's time for a broader view of the world.

A global portfolio

The good news for investors is that the premium valuations of the US equity market are largely a local phenomenon. While bonds are expensive, i.e. real rates are low, throughout the world, most stock markets are materially cheaper than the United States.

The MSCI World ex-US Index, an index of developed markets outside of the United States, is trading at a discount to its 20-year average and at a cheaper valuation than was the case a year ago. Japanese stocks, most emerging markets, and large parts of Europe still appear reasonably priced. Most of these markets have simply not enjoyed the same grinding multiple expansion that has defined the US bull market (see Chart 4.4).

Chart 4.4: Cyclically adjusted P/E ratio (CAPE) of European equities

Source: BlackRock, Bloomberg, April 2017.

Cheaper valuations outside of the US suggest the prospect for better returns will stem from a more diversified portfolio. A similar argument holds on the bond side. While traditional bonds in the US, Europe and Japan have never been more expensive, bond yields look a bit more enticing in select emerging markets. While riskier, they do offer the prospect of much higher yields and in some cases diversification. Chart 4.5 shows the recent history of 10-year yields in Brazil, as an example.

The takeaway is that while the bull market is long in the tooth, not all asset classes have benefited equally across all geographies. US stocks and traditional bonds have performed exceptionally well. As a result, these asset classes are expensive and arguably offer lower returns going forward. Fortunately, there are still many market segments globally that are reasonably priced, and in a few cases even cheap. Going forward, investors need to be more willing to embrace global investment opportunities rather than relying on investing in the US assets that have performed well in recent years.

Chart 4.5: 10-year Brazilian bond yields (%)

Source: BlackRock, Bloomberg, April 2017.

Key concepts: geographic diversification

- Recent performance for US stocks and bonds has been unusually good.
- This period of stellar performance is unlikely to continue over the long term. The very factors that drove US stock and bond performance are unrepeatable. At the very least, this suggests lower returns going forward.
- Fortunately, other global markets are more reasonably priced. Investors should use this as an opportunity to diversify.

Living inside the matrix

If investors are to embrace diversification, this still leaves the question of how to allocate to new investments and different geographies. The goal, as described, is to find asset classes with a low or even negative correlation to the rest of the portfolio. Fortunately, there is an efficient way to do this.

Measuring the correlation of two assets is relatively easy and can be expressed with a single number. However, the process becomes more cumbersome when you're trying to describe the co-movement of multiple assets. This is where investors will want to become familiar with the concept of the *covariance matrix.*

The covariance matrix is a relatively simple concept and an indispensable tool for asset allocators. The covariance matrix provides a succinct method for measuring the risk of each asset and their co-movement relative to each other.

The reason the matrix is so valuable is that there is a well-established body of knowledge surrounding matrices, known as linear algebra. It is this tool that helps build portfolios using a technique known as *mean-variance optimization* (this is the subject of Chapter 7).

Before turning to the role of the matrix in a full-blown optimization it is worth considering how it can be used in assessing risk. Chart 4.6 shows a simplified example of a matrix representing six asset classes: US equities, non-US developed market equities, emerging market equities, long-dated US Treasury bonds, gold and cash.

The numbers on the diagonal represent the risk of the asset class. It is worth noting that in this example, risk is represented using standard deviation and correlation. This is done as by now you will hopefully be familiar with the concept (see Chapter 3). In practice, the covariance matrix would, as the name implies, use the variance and covariance of returns. The variance is the square of the standard deviation and the covariance is the correlation multiplied by the product of the standard deviations of the two variables.

Chart 4.6: Asset class correlation matrix

	S&P 500	International Developed	Emerging Markets	US Treasuries +20 years	Gold	Cash
S&P 500	0.15	0.75	0.6	-0.3	-0.15	0
International Developed	0.75	0.18	0.55	-0.1	-0.05	0.01
Emerging Markets	0.6	0.55	0.22	-0.3	0.01	0
U.S. Treasuries +20 years	-0.3	-0.1	-0.3	0.05	0.1	0.05
Gold	-0.15	-0.05	0.01	0.1	0.25	-0.1
Cash	0	0.01	0	0.05	-0.1	0.01

Source: Bloomberg, April 2017.

In terms of the mechanics of generating a covariance or correlation matrix, most financial software, such as a Bloomberg terminal, can do this automatically once you enter a list of assets. It is also relatively easy to generate a small covariance or correlation matrix on a spreadsheet.

To generate a correlation matrix on a spreadsheet, the first step is to obtain a time series of returns for each asset class in your universe. The returns can be calculated using daily, weekly or monthly data. Next you need to calculate the standard deviation of returns, represented on the diagonal of the matrix, for each asset class. Most simple models will use approximately five years of data. The final step is to compute a correlation for each pair of assets, with those numbers populating either the lower half or the upper half of the matrix. All the calculations, standard deviation and correlation, are standard functions on any spreadsheet program.

Returning to the above example, the exercise in creating a correlation matrix illustrates a few key concepts. As discussed previously, stocks are generally much riskier than bonds or cash. And while gold tends to be diversifying, on its own it is a volatile asset class with an expected risk higher than that of bonds or stocks.

The rest of the numbers, sometimes referred to as the off-diagonals, represent the correlation between different pairs of assets. As you may notice, all the correlations are represented twice. For example, in this example the correlation between US stocks and international stocks is high, at approximately 0.75.

What this means is that US equities and stocks in Europe and Japan tend to move together. In contrast, the correlation of US stocks with US Treasury bonds is negative, suggesting that stocks and bonds have a modest tendency to move in the opposite direction.

The covariance matrix is most powerful as an input into a portfolio optimization. That said, it still serves a purpose even if you don't actually use a formal portfolio construction process. Even on its own, the covariance matrix provides a simple way of representing the expected risk in a portfolio. The matrix succinctly summarizes risk from two key perspectives: the risk of each individual asset as well as the extent to which the different assets do or don't move together.

Shifting correlations

One trap to avoid, not just when estimating risk but also when estimating returns, is to take precision too far. A covariance matrix seems like a very rigorous and precise way to measure risk. It is, as far as it goes. The problem is that you're using historical numbers to forecast the future.

As previously discussed, historical risk numbers are useful and provide a rough approximation of what risk is likely to look like in the future. But the emphasis needs to be on the word *rough*.

As with returns, correlations move around a lot. Measuring a correlation over the past few years, which is what is generally represented in a covariance matrix, may not be indicative of the next few years. In fact, you can be sure that future risk or correlations will never exactly match what is estimated in the covariance matrix.

The reason is that the covariance matrix is calculated using historical returns. There are simple ways to do this and more sophisticated methods, but regardless of the level of complexity, all methods look at historical returns and try to draw inferences about the future. The obvious problem is that history rarely repeats itself. Estimates of risk may be correct in an ordinal sense, i.e. stocks are more volatile than bonds, but the actual measurement will never perfectly represent future conditions.

Stocks which seem well behaved during a bull market suddenly become much more volatile during bear markets. Bonds, while lower-risk assets than stocks, can inflict losses when central banks are raising interest rates.

Correlations vary as well. As demonstrated in Chapter 1, since the late 1970s stock/bond correlations have been as high as 0.60, indicating a tendency for stocks and bonds to move together. At other times the correlation has been as low as -0.4, suggesting that bonds tend to rise when stocks drop. Correlations, like returns and risk, are a function of market conditions. When market conditions change, correlations change.

The takeaway is to consider the current environment. To the extent it resembles the past, and is likely to continue, the risk estimates contained in the covariance matrix provide a reasonable approximation of future risk.

The problem comes when the world changes. If the covariance matrix was estimated during the past five years of growth and you're on the cusp of a recession, you have a problem. Under this scenario, assets that behaved one way during an economic expansion are likely to behave very differently when the economy is contracting. The same holds for a change in inflation, interest rates or general risk appetite.

While there is no way to get to a perfect estimate of risk, it is worth asking a simple question: is the future environment likely to resemble the recent past? If the answer is no, it's better to estimate the covariance matrix over a different period – preferably one that includes the type of market environment you expect in the future.

A simple example of this exercise relates to interest rates. What if an investor, in the process of trying to estimate risk, believed that the bull market in bonds was finished? Instead of a multi-decade period of falling rates we were now entering a period when interest rates will rise year-after-year. In thinking about risk, this investor would be well served to go back and observe risk estimates from the late 1970s or 1994, one of the last periods when interest rates rose unexpectedly. This exercise might suggest that volatility and correlation look different in an environment of rising rates versus one characterized by falling rates.

Going their own way

The benefit of a risk estimate, whether through a covariance matrix or other method, is that it forces you to have an explicit estimate of risk. Investors spend most of their time forecasting returns. The risk side of the equation merits more attention. Different risk and correlation estimates, even with the same return assumptions, can lead to very different portfolios.

A recent example illustrates the importance of correlation in building portfolios: the drop in inter-market correlations. One of the numerous challenges for investors since the financial crisis is that many markets have moved together. This is another reason investors have become more skeptical when it comes to diversification. When most stocks are doing the same thing at the same time, adding another correlated position compounds risk rather than mitigates it.

The reason that markets have had a greater tendency to move together in recent years is open to debate. Some attribute this trend to a more interconnected, global economy. Other theories include the growing dominance of central banks, which cause investors across the world to act in a similar fashion. Whatever the cause, this tendency is starting to shift. This provides a good example of how correlations move over time.

During the past year or two, the correlation between various markets has started to drop. As Chart 4.7 illustrates, the correlation between US and non-US equity markets fell from approximately 0.85 in early 2016 to approximately 0.5 in the summer of 2017. This suggests that relative to a few years ago there is more benefit to owning markets outside your home country, as they should provide more diversification.

Chart 4.7: Rolling correlation of US and non-US equity markets

Source: BlackRock, Bloomberg.

The above example helps illustrate why investors should pay attention to the risk estimates in the covariance matrix. In this instance, investors may want to use a covariance matrix that emphasizes more recent data, rather than the very long term. This way, the risk estimates will reflect the recent decrease in correlations between equity markets.

While investors intuitively know what to do when they expect higher returns – buy more – it is not always as obvious how to change an allocation based on correlation. The topic will be covered in more detail in Chapter 7, but for now suffice to say that a few rules of thumb can help guide your allocation.

First, while most people focus on return, i.e. own more of what you think will go up the most, holdings should also scale based on both risk and correlation. As a general rule, if you have two assets with the same expected return, own more of the asset with lower expected risk. The second rule of thumb applies to correlation. Building robust portfolios requires owning assets that don't all do the same thing at the same time.

This translates into owning more of those assets with a low or negative correlation to the rest of your portfolio.

A simple example should help illustrate the concept. Imagine a very basic portfolio made up of stocks, bonds and gold. How much the investor would hold in bonds will be in large part determined by their correlation with stocks. As bonds typically return less than stocks, the investor would want to hold bonds primarily as a way to lower the portfolio's risk. As discussed previously, bonds lower portfolio risk as they are both less risky than stocks and often negatively correlated with stocks. As a simple rule the investor would own more bonds during those periods when she expected stock/bond correlations to be particularly negative.

A similar argument holds for gold. As I demonstrate in Chapter 7, an investor can assume a very low return for gold and still be justified in holding 5% of a portfolio in the precious metal. The key assumption is not the return expectation, it is the expectation for *correlations*. An investor owns more gold when she believes that gold will go up when the rest of the portfolio is going down. How much gold is held also scales with how negative a correlation is expected between gold and the rest of the portfolio.

Has diversification traditionally worked?

Theory aside, many investors look at the past seven or eight years and remain skeptical. Yes, correlations may be a bit lower than they were, but the world is still interconnected.

In addition, US investors often make the not totally irrational argument that US markets lead. If US stocks go down, other markets are likely to follow. To paraphrase an old expression, "when the US catches a cold the rest of the world gets the flu." In which case, why accept the marginal risk from international markets?

A bit of history is helpful in answering this objection. Non-US developed markets, such as Europe, Japan and Canada, did well in the 1980s, particularly Japan. For those old enough to remember, there was a time when Japan seemed to be on the verge of taking over the world.

Weekly news magazines would run nervous headlines on the latest Japanese acquisition of a US trophy property.

Much has changed during the past three decades. Since the early 1990s, Japan has struggled with economic stagnation and a secular bear market. At the same time, US stocks have trounced the rest of the developed world. Since 1990, the S&P 500 has produced an average annual total return, including both price appreciation as well as dividends, of nearly 11%.

In contrast, the average return to the MSCI World ex-US index has been a bit below 8%. As Chart 4.8 illustrates, it is hard to argue for international diversification when the US equity market has consistently outperformed during a span of nearly three decades.

Chart 4.8: Performance of S&P 500 and MSCI World ex-US (%)

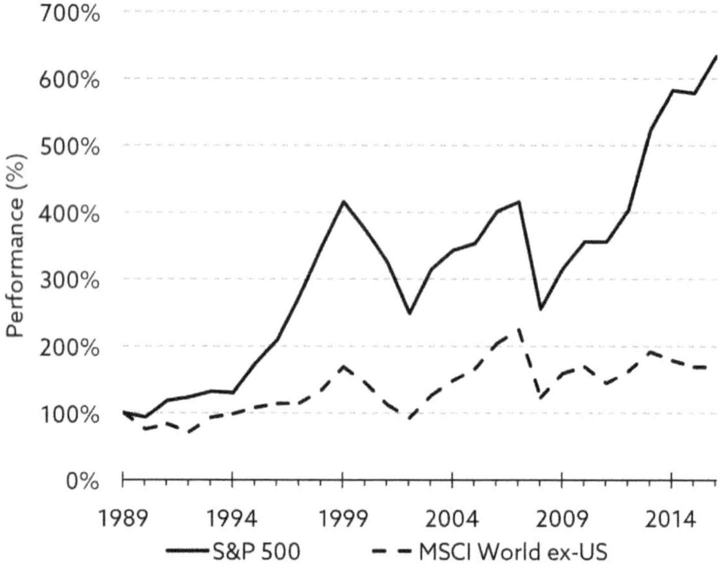

Source: Bloomberg, April 2017.

Look beneath the surface, however, and it is less clear that the past will be prologue to the future. During that three-decade period, much of the underperformance of non-US markets can be attributed specifically to Japanese stocks.

Despite better performance in recent years, Japanese equities have never recovered their former glory. Having peaked at nearly 40,000 in late 1989, the Nikkei 225 is still languishing at roughly half of that level (see Chart 4.9). In fact, Japanese stocks have effectively been stuck in a broad trading range, between 10,000 and 20,000 on the Nikkei, for approximately a quarter century!

Chart 4.9: Nikkei 225, 1989–2017

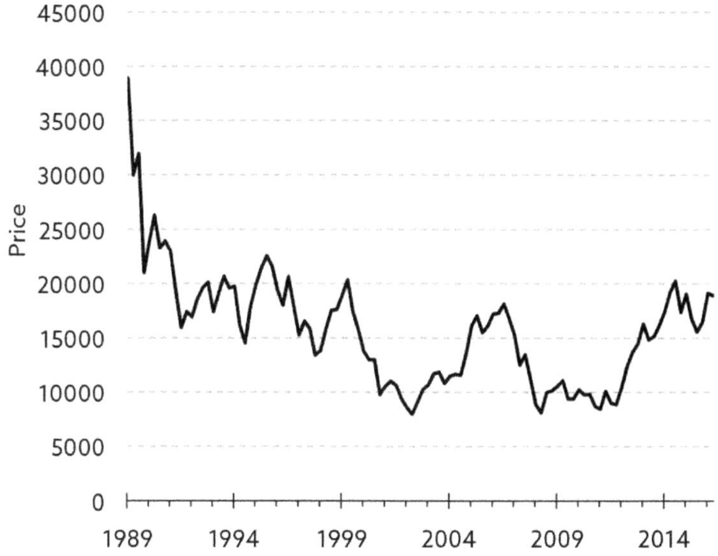

Source: Bloomberg, April 2017.

The long-term stagnation in Japanese equities explains a good deal of the underperformance of non-US equities, particularly developed markets. At its peak, Japan accounted for approximately 40% of the market cap of global equities and obviously an even higher percentage of non-US equities. To the extent Japanese equities struggled, by definition non-US developed markets would struggle given Japan's outsize influence on international indices.

More recently the situation has started to change. Unlike the case 25-years ago, today Japan accounts for less than 8% of global equity markets. This means that today whatever happens to Japan, good or bad, has a much smaller impact on global equity markets than during the late 1980s or early 1990s.

Another thing that has changed has been the rise of emerging markets (EMs) as an investable asset class. Chapter 2 highlighted the competitive returns of this asset class, albeit at the cost of higher volatility. As emerging markets grow as a percentage of global equity markets this should lead to a greater diversification benefit; EM stocks tend to have a lower correlation with US stocks than stocks in Europe or Japan.

For example, compare the total returns of two blended portfolios since 2001. A global portfolio, including emerging markets, starts to look much more competitive.

Since the start of 2001, the S&P 500 has produced an average total return of 7.1%. During that same period the MSCI All-Country World Index (ACWI), a comprehensive global equity index including the United States, international developed markets and emerging markets, has returned 6.5% (see Chart 4.10).

While international markets were still a drag on performance, the gap is modest and much reduced on what we saw in Chart 4.8 for the period since 1990 (note, I've used the ACWI in this chart to capture the impact from emerging markets). The fact that international markets, notably Japan, have exerted a less negative influence recently is a function of several factors: Japan is now a much smaller portion of global markets, Japanese stocks have actually performed better in recent years, and emerging markets have been additive over the long term.

Chart 4.10: S&P 500 vs ACWI annual total return

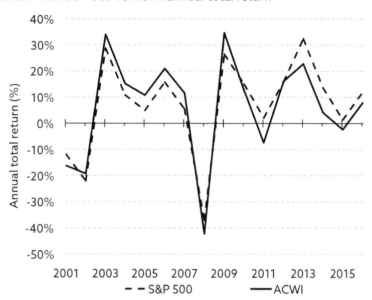

Source: Bloomberg, April 2017.

Don't exclude emerging markets

Looking at a broader definition of global markets, one that includes EMs, is important in making the case for international diversification. Not only do the returns look better when EMs are included, but adding them to the mix also adds to the diversification benefit. Emerging markets tend to be less correlated with developed markets than developed markets are with each other. This is particularly true when considering US market returns versus those in emerging countries.

Chart 4.11 helps illustrate the relationship. The chart looks at five-year correlations, based on monthly data, between three pairs: US equities (S&P 500) versus the ex-US developed markets (MSCI World), US equities versus emerging markets (MSCI emerging markets) and the ex-US developed markets versus emerging markets.

Chart 4.11: 60-month rolling correlations

Source: Bloomberg, April 2017.

There are a few key points to highlight. First and foremost, equity markets tend to be highly correlated with each other. While global markets do not move in lockstep, they tend to move in the same direction, at least most of the time. Unlike government bonds or gold, other major equity markets are unlikely to move in the opposite direction from the investor's home country for any length of time.

Looking at the data, during the past 28 years the average correlation between the major equity indices – US, non-US developed markets and emerging markets – has been 0.74. While this does not represent perfect correlation, it is still a relatively high number. In other words, while diversification across international equity markets makes sense, it will not protect investors, particularly during periods of volatility, as well as allocating to other asset classes. This is the argument for always having a multi-asset class portfolio.

The second, related point is that markets have tended to become more correlated over time. While correlations have fallen somewhat in recent years, they are still on average materially higher than they were in the mid-1990s. This should probably not come as a surprise. The global economy and investors within it are more interconnected than they were 25 years ago.

Still, the third point argues for EMs providing some marginal diversification. While stocks tend to move together, developed markets have a higher propensity to co-move than developed and emerging markets. Based on the five-year correlation metric described above, the average correlation between the United States and other developed markets has been a little under 0.80. The average correlation between developed and emerging markets has been approximately 0.73. Not a big difference, but enough to lend some support to the argument for EMs as a diversifier.

The argument is stronger for US-based investors, where the average correlation has been 0.70, even lower in recent years, than for investors in Europe or Japan. Arguably the lower correlation with US equities reflects the fact that the US economy and stock market are more domestically driven. In contrast, Europe and Japan are more dominated by global trade, making them more correlated with emerging markets.

What to do about currency

While international markets provide diversification, they also provide more risk. Much of that marginal risk comes from owning stocks or bonds that are denominated in another currency. This is foreign exchange (f/x) risk. The fluctuations in that currency, apart from the fluctuations in the underlying stock or bond, provide another source of volatility.

When an investor based in the United States buys stocks in Europe or Japan, they are not only exposed to the risk of the stock but also of the euro or yen. If the stock price goes up but the yen weakens against the dollar, returns will be negatively impacted.

Over the long term, this may not have a huge impact as currency effects tend to equal out, but it can have a profound impact in the short term. For investors who want to invest internationally but don't want to wear the risk associated with the foreign currency exposure there is a simple solution: own funds that hedge out part or all of the f/x risk.

Many active fund managers will do this as a matter of course. Alternatively, investors can increasingly buy ETFs that own international markets but hedge out the f/x exposure. As a result, the return received by the investor is the equivalent in local dollars. An investor that buys a yen hedged equity ETF will receive the same returns as a local Japanese investor, minus the cost of hedging.

This may be a particularly good idea in international bond markets. The simple reason for this is that currency volatility is often greater than the underlying volatility of the bond. As a result, an unhedged position in a foreign bond or bond fund is more of a bet on the direction of the currency than the attractiveness of the bond. If the investor doesn't have a strong view on the currency, it's better to own a fund or ETF that hedges that exposure.

Trading currency is an art in itself. Currencies present a particular challenge as, unlike stocks, bonds or real estate, it is hard to value the dollar versus the euro or the pound versus the yen. If an investor feels they have an opinion and skill forecasting currency moves, currency risk provides another potential source of return. For everyone else, and in particular those concerned about short-term volatility, mutual funds or ETFs that limit the f/x exposure provide a solution.

The loophole

Investors often put forth a few arguments, most of them defensible, against diversification. Many would start with the simple argument that as markets have become increasingly correlated, why bother. This has been particularly true over the past decade as stock markets, along with other financial markets, have moved in lockstep to the tune of central banks.

Many also point to the added risk from taking on currency exposure. To go outside of one's home market means to accept f/x risk. Most academic research suggests that currency markets are hard to predict. Furthermore, unlike holding stocks or bonds there is little evidence that holding a foreign currency position should lead to a positive return over time. Again then, why bother?

The third, and perhaps most powerful, argument is that diversification does not work in the short term. Markets have and will continue to experience corrections and bear markets. In bear markets, most equity markets, along with high-yield and emerging market bonds, are likely to sink together. During these periods, other than owning safe-haven bonds, cash and perhaps gold, few assets provided much ballast. In some instances, such as the short-lived taper tantrum of 2013, even Treasuries and gold failed to provide any comfort.

Finally, for many US-based investors there has been no need to diversify. A simple domestic stock/bond mix has produced stellar returns and a deceptively smooth ride. Why venture abroad?

However, diversification works in the long term. Over a multi-decade horizon, diversification can make a difference, not necessarily in terms of higher returns but in terms of better risk-adjusted returns.

By combining different geographies and assets the investor arrives at a more efficient, robust portfolio. A portfolio with higher returns for a given level of risk than any one or two asset classes are likely to produce.

Key concepts: diversification and correlation

➼ Diversification ultimately relies on finding securities and asset classes that don't rise or fall together.

➼ Diversification does not work in the short term or during periods of market volatility. That said, it is the best way to improve risk-adjusted returns over the long term.

➼ A covariance matrix is an efficient tool for tracking the correlation of different assets and the riskiness of each individual asset class.

➼ In recent years, the benefits of diversification have been less evident as international markets have tended to move together. As we move further away from the financial crisis, this appears to be changing. To the extent this continues, it will restore some of the value to international diversification.

5

A New Lens:
How Factors Drive
Performance

THUS FAR THE discussion has revolved around the traditional building blocks of a portfolio. These are generally defined as stocks, bonds and cash. Some investors will add more esoteric asset classes to the mix: commodities, real estate and occasionally alternatives, such as hedge funds. Whether held directly, through a mutual fund or through an ETF, this is the traditional taxonomy investors use when thinking about the various pieces of their portfolio.

There is another way to view a portfolio. Rather than thinking about a collection of assets, a portfolio can also be described as a collection of *factors*. Factors are underlying drivers of returns. Andrew Ang, one of the fathers of factor investing (and a colleague of mine), likens factors to nutrients. While food can take many forms, the underlying nutrients ultimately provide the nourishment.

Factors impact assets, regardless of the particular asset class. For example, as discussed earlier, *economic growth* impacts stocks; growth is also a driver of returns for various other asset classes, including high-yield bonds, real estate and many commodities.

Value provides another example of a factor that cuts across various asset classes. Whether stocks or bonds, many investors focus on building a portfolio based on what they perceive to be value, i.e. buying what is cheap and avoiding what is expensive. Buying inexpensive assets, and accepting the volatility that often accompanies this style, provides an additional premium for investors.

A third example is *momentum* – the practice of favoring securities that are rising. This is based on the observation that investors have historically received a premium for holding securities that demonstrate positive momentum.

All three of these examples – economic growth, value and momentum – are factors.

In addition to these three factors, there are also less obvious drivers of returns. In recent years investors have been embracing low volatility stocks, a style often referred to as minimum volatility. Historically, this has been another example of a style factor, similar to value and momentum, but perhaps not yet as popular.

A different prism

Approaching a portfolio from the perspective of factors is known as *factor investing*. The approach has several advantages. As highlighted repeatedly, describing an asset as a stock or a bond ignores the many intra-asset class differences. Not all stocks and bonds are created equal. Under certain circumstances some stocks can behave more like bonds and some bonds like stocks. Factor investing helps explain that seemingly odd behavior by uncovering the underlying drivers of returns.

There is a second advantage. Occasionally a theme, such as momentum, is the primary driver of market performance. In these instances factors are arguably a better way to explain underlying market behavior that may cut across different asset classes.

Finally, certain style factors confer a premium. In other words, the returns to these factors have beaten the returns available from more traditional indices. Investors willing to tilt their portfolio towards these factors stand to improve their risk-adjusted performance.

For anyone responsible for building portfolios, a basic appreciation of factor investing is a must. Factors provide a different but critically important way to understand markets. Think of them as another prism through which to view an investment portfolio. Rather than just considering an allocation of assets, also start to think in terms of a collection of factors.

What lies beneath

By training and habit most of us have been conditioned to view the market from the perspective of asset class performance. We turn on the financial news and the day's market is described in terms of how stocks, bonds and perhaps gold did that day. This is how the market gets framed.

Thinking about factors requires investors to change their perspective and rethink what drives returns. Apart from the specifics of stocks, bonds or other asset classes, there are these underlying drivers; they often go underappreciated but are nevertheless crucial. These are the undercurrents that ultimately drive the direction of any portfolio.

As an example, consider the performance of any stock. One way to think about a stock's performance is to focus on the fundamentals of the company. For many stock pickers, a stock's long-term performance is a function of its business prospects and intrinsic value.

Fundamentals may well win out over the long term – good companies with successful business models tend to produce better returns – but the short term is different. In the short term, stocks are driven by investor preferences, which often have little to do with the fundamentals of a company. Sometimes investors favor more defensive firms. At other times value or momentum is more in vogue. In aggregate, these and other factors account for a significant portion of the variation in returns.

One risk to rule them all

Modern factor theory posits numerous factors, from economic ones to investment styles. In aggregate, these factors drive returns. But what if you envisioned a world with only a single factor: the market. While an incomplete description of the world, the single-factor model is useful as an introduction to how factors work in practice.

As described earlier, the biggest factor that investors need to be aware of is the market. Stocks do not move in isolation. Regardless of a company's fundamentals or a stock's characteristics, all stocks are influenced by the market.

The theory that encapsulates this view is the capital asset pricing model (CAPM). The theory posits just two types of risk: specific risk, unique to that particular stock; and systematic risk, which represents the market risk. While you can diversify a portfolio to eliminate specific risk, no matter how hard you try you cannot avoid market risk. That is the price of entry.

Despite some mildly daunting math, the CAPM presents a simple model of the world. The premium you receive for a stock or index is simply a function of its beta to the market and the premium investors are demanding to own stocks. While subsequent research demonstrated that there is more than just one factor that drives markets, the concept is still useful. And in fact, that market does have a significant influence on just about any stock.

Take a simple example. During a five-year period Apple's (AAPL) weekly performance was in large part determined by the performance of the broader stock market, as measured by the S&P 500. This can be demonstrated by referring to Chart 5.1, which shows weekly changes in the price of Apple compared to weekly change in the price of the S&P 500. As the equation shows, Apple generally moved with the market, only a bit more so. This is evident in the estimated beta of 1.06; for every 1% move in S&P 500, Apple advanced approximately 1.06%. Put differently, changes in the price of Apple were largely driven by changes in the broader stock market.

During this period, lots of things happened to Apple. The iPad became a ubiquitous corporate accessory, the iPad mini was launched, as were multiple versions of the iPhone. Apart from the direct impact on a few key suppliers and competitors, all of these events were idiosyncratic to Apple. Yet, the performance of the broader market still exerted a strong influence on what happened to Apple on any given week. In short, the market matters, even to an iconic company like Apple.

Chart 5.1: Apple (AAPL) beta vs S&P 500, April 2012–April 2017

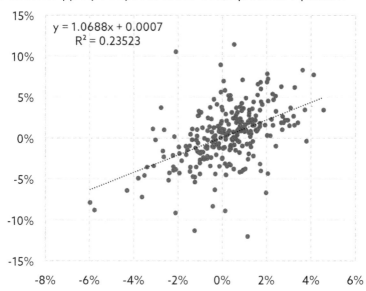

Source: Bloomberg, April 2017.

A multi-factor world

While the CAPM is a useful starting point, it is perhaps an overly simplistic one. In reality the world is complex and can't be reduced to a single factor. Subsequent financial theories sought to address this shortcoming. The arbitrage pricing theory (APT), introduced in 1976, envisioned a world in which there was not one but multiple factors that impacted returns. These factors include not only the market but also additional factors such as a company's relative value and size.

Over time academics have posited other factors. As it turns out, securities are influenced by myriad influences that stretch much beyond whether a particular company is cheap or small. Many of these factors have nothing at all to do with the underlying company. Factors such as momentum or low volatility are driven by how the stock behaves, rather than the firm itself. That behavior is in turn driven by investor preferences, which tend to change over time.

At any given point in time, investors may display a strong preference for one style factor over another. Recent history provides a good illustration. The 12 months from early summer 2016 to early summer 2017 demonstrate just how fickle investors can be in their preferences.

During the first six-month period, the back half of 2016, investors were recovering from the pessimism of earlier in that year. Markets got off to a rough start in 2016, with investor fear driven by pessimism over the economy. However, by mid-summer investors were becoming more sanguine about the economic outlook. Sentiment and markets got an added boost in late 2016. In the 12 hours following the US Presidential election, investors abruptly decided that a Trump administration, unleashing tax cuts and deregulation, would in fact be good for the market.

During this period investors did what they typically do when becoming more positive on the economy: they bought cyclical companies and value stocks. These are perceived to benefit most from a strengthening economy. At the same time, investors sold safer, more defensive companies. When people are expecting better times, why play it safe? As a result, the back half of 2016 was a great time for value and a more difficult time for low volatility companies.

Beginning in early 2017, the situation abruptly reversed. Suddenly investors were less confident in the Trump administration's ability to deliver. The evidence supporting a pickup in growth and inflation became mixed. Oil prices were slipping. In this environment, cyclical companies like banks and energy firms seemed less certain.

Instead, investors reverted back to an old playbook. More modest expectations about growth and inflation suggest emphasizing different characteristics. This is when growth stocks started to outperform again. In an environment of slow growth investors are more willing to pay a premium for companies that can generate faster earnings growth, regardless of the economic environment.

Investors also re-embraced dividend stocks. Out of favor in late 2016, companies with generous yields sprung back to life in early 2017. The reason: interest rates unexpectedly started to drop again. As discussed previously, when rates are falling, particularly from such low levels, investors will typically put a premium on a high and reliable dividend yield.

This one-year period provides a good illustration of the importance of factors to performance. Investor preferences change, often suddenly, based on their perception of growth, inflation and their willingness to embrace risk. To the extent a stock has a characteristic that is in favor during these periods, it is more likely to rise than a stock that lacks that characteristic.

The factor zoo

As with asset classes, factors can be organized by type. While factors come in many shapes and sizes, they generally fit into two broad categories: *macro factors* and *style factors*. Macro factors are underlying economic drivers. These are facets of the real economy, such as economic growth or inflation. Investors are paid a premium for accepting these risks. This is why stocks or even bonds generally produce higher returns than cash. Investors need to be compensated for taking the macro risks associated with these asset classes.

Examples of macro factors include economic growth, inflation and real rates. There are also less obvious factors such as exposure to emerging markets or liquidity, i.e. the premium investors earn for owning non-liquid investments such as real estate or a hedge fund.

The other main factor category is style. Style factors represent characteristics of a security, such as momentum or quality. These attributes distinguish securities within an asset class. In addition to value and momentum, there are other style factors such as volatility and size. There are also style factors particular to the bond market, such as carry or the curve.

In the past, many of these style factors were hard to observe, unless you were a professional money manager able to construct customized baskets of stocks with certain characteristics. Thankfully, in recent years it has become easier and far less abstract to talk about factor performance.

There are now a number of factor ETFs. These instruments offer direct exposure to securities with these characteristics.

Economic factors

Going into a bit more detail, macro factors are important to understand because these are drivers that impact virtually every asset class. Stocks, bonds, commodities or real estate are all impacted, albeit to varying degrees, by what happens in the real economy. Regardless of the specific stock and bond an investor owns, their portfolio is subject to certain big macro trends, such as the rate of economic growth or inflation.

Economic growth tends to be pervasive in its impact. One of the reasons stocks generally return more than bonds is that owning stocks entails more economic risk, specifically to growth. A bondholder has a guaranteed payment, assuming the issuer does not default. An equity investor has only a residual claim on a company's resources. If there are insufficient earnings the company may cut its dividend. In the event the company goes bankrupt, which is much more likely during a recession, bondholders get paid first.

Even under less dire circumstances, equity holders bear significant economic risk. Ask any CEO how easy it is to grow earnings during a downturn. Stocks simply entail more economic risk than bonds. Therefore, the return *premium* for owning a stock should be higher in order to compensate investors for that risk.

Exposure to macro factors also matters intra-asset class. As discussed previously, high-yield bonds are more sensitive to economic growth than either Treasury bonds or investment-grade debt. This is because high-yield issuers are riskier companies. Sometimes the company is younger or smaller. In other instances, the issuing firm already has a significant amount of debt, making it more vulnerable in the event of a recession or slowdown.

In all these examples, the company has a smaller margin for error than a larger, more established or less indebted firm. High-yield issuers are more dependent on a good economy to ensure that earnings will be sufficient to cover the cost of servicing its debt. Therefore, high-yield issues tend to be more exposed to economic growth than other issuers of debt.

Real estate is another example of an asset class exposed to growth. It is easier to raise rents when the economy is doing well and inflation is rising. Conversely, during an economic downturn renters are more likely to ask for concessions or attempt to break their leases.

Finally, there are commodities. Most commodities, gold being an exception, are impacted by industrial demand, which is ultimately driven by the level of economic growth. This is true for industrial metals, such as copper, oil or even natural gas, For example, during an economic boom there is generally more building, which in turn influences the demand for copper. Likewise, people drive more during good times and less during a recession. Miles driven impact the demand for oil. In general, most commodities will have some non-trivial exposure to economic growth.

What ties all of these examples together is their significant exposure to the growth factor. Stocks, high-yield debt, real estate and commodities are four very distinct asset classes, with very different fundamentals. Yet, they are all driven to a greater or lesser extent by the common factor of the economy. In return, investors expect a premium over other, safer investments for accepting exposure to this particular risk factor.

Exposures vary

While all of the asset classes just mentioned are exposed to growth, the extent varies. An industrial, highly cyclical stock is more levered to growth than a real estate trust (REIT) that rents real estate to hospitals. While they both share a common risk factor, the *level* of exposure will be different.

This is evident when examining their performance during and after the great recession. While all four asset classes moved in a similar direction, the magnitude varied (see Chart 5.2).

Chart 5.2: Cyclical asset performance

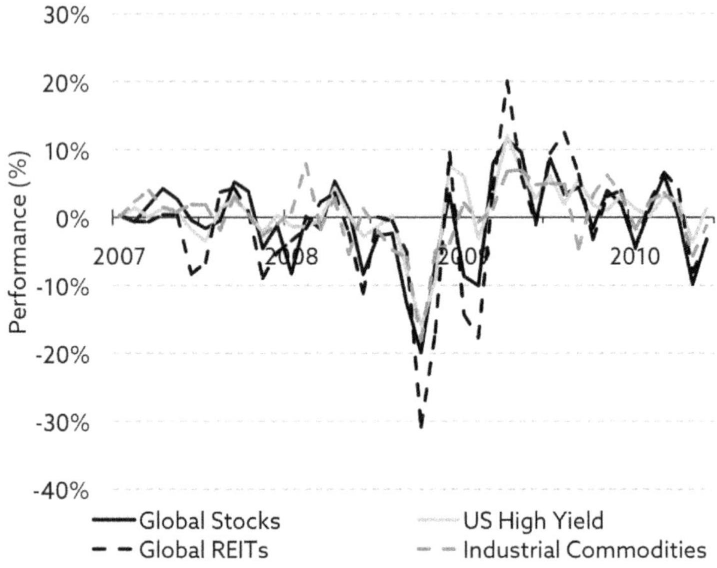

Source: Bloomberg, April 2017.

According to the US National Bureau of Economic Research, the US recession began in December 2007 and ended in June of 2009, lasting 18 months. Looking at the period defined as the year before and after the great recession, the recession impacted each of the four asset classes to varying degrees. For those most leveraged to economic growth, the results were not pretty.

The economic impact was greatest for real estate and industrial commodities and least for high-yield. This is a somewhat intuitive result. High-yield, while economically sensitive, is also a bond. While the equity-like exposure will suffer from the drop in growth, the bond-like characteristics help offset that tendency. In contrast, real estate and commodities are directly tied to economic activity and end demand. It makes sense that their exposure to changes in growth should be the greatest.

The above example illustrates a few key points. Economic factors cut across all asset classes. They are a common driver of returns. That said, the impact differs from asset class to asset class and from security to security. Still, when there are abrupt changes in the economy, particularly negative ones such as a sharp drop in growth or a quick spike in inflation, beware. Asset class diversification is not enough if all of your assets have the same exposure to that factor. To combat this, the investor needs to build a diversified portfolio with assets that carry *different* factor exposures, such as stocks and government bonds.

Investing with style

If macro factors are best defined by economic characteristics, style factors relate to how people invest. These factors help explain the dispersion of returns within an asset class. Many of the previous examples, such as value and momentum, are style factors. These styles have the added distinction of being associated with a positive risk premium, i.e. the investor is rewarded over the long term for emphasizing these styles. Investors should consider tilting their portfolios towards securities and industries that display these characteristics.

The important thing about style factors is that they are applicable, to a greater or lesser degree, across sectors and markets. Looking at equities as an example, stocks representing companies in very different industries may still have similar exposures to a particular style.

Stocks of both banks and energy often display value characteristics. While companies in these two industries have completely different business models and fundamentals, at the time of writing in mid-2017 many companies in both industries display a similar characteristic: they are relatively cheap.

This seems strange. After all, what do a regional bank and a mid-cap oil exploration and production company have in common? The answer is that at certain points in the economic cycle what investors really want is not a bank or an oil company but a cheap stock, which is an attribute that both types of stocks currently share. At certain points in the market cycle that shared characteristic is more important than the particulars of their respective industries. During these periods, often when the economy is coming out of a recession, investors are willing and even anxious to take on the risk associated with value stocks.

Another example is momentum. Momentum stocks, as the name implies, tend to trend. These are stocks that have a tendency to move in the same direction, either up or down, for extended periods of time. While there is no single time frame to measure the trend, most measures of momentum are based on a year of returns.

Technology companies during the tech bubble are a good example of stocks exhibiting strong momentum. They went up on Tuesday largely because they rose on Monday. As more and more investors chased these names it reinforced the trend. That is, of course, until the trend ended. At which point the tech stocks demonstrated an equally impressive tendency to trend, just in the opposite direction.

A third, somewhat more abstract example of an equity style factor is quality. Unlike momentum, which is defined by how the stock trades, quality is about the underlying company. Companies that exhibit quality are generally more stable and reliable than the average firm. Generally these firms share certain characteristics: they are consistently profitable, generate a reliable earnings stream and have relatively low debt.

Quality companies can be found in most industries but they are particularly prevalent in large, established technology or financial companies, healthcare or consumer staples. These are all businesses that tend to generate profits regardless of what the economy is doing. During recessions or periods of volatility, investors often embrace this characteristic.

Over time the performance of these investment styles can diverge, depending on investor preference. Momentum is favored when volatility is low. Value tends to be most in demand when the economy is accelerating, resulting in faster earnings growth for most companies, not just the high-flying growth names. Quality tends to work best when people are most afraid. During these periods, investors prefer stocks with a particular attribute: they are less likely to blow up.

These dynamics have been on display in recent years. Chart 5.3 tracks the recent performance of these three equity style factors. Most recently, given low volatility and modest growth, momentum has been the investor darling. Less favoured has been value, which has underperformed momentum and quality stocks during the past four years. This dynamic fits into the broader pattern described above: value struggles when growth is modest.

Chart 5.3: US equity style factor ETF returns

Source: Bloomberg, iShares, April 2017.

Style premium

While at any given time investors may favor growth over momentum or value over quality, over the long term these styles have all been additive. In other words, they have historically produced returns in excess of the broader stock market. Tilting towards value, momentum, quality, size (size being defined as a larger weighting to small companies) and low volatility companies has been rewarded.

Of these tilts, arguably the one with the longest pedigree is value. Historically, although admittedly not recently, value has offered better returns than simply buying and holding the broader market. This is not hard to understand.

Cheaper stocks have more room to rise. To the extent investors in a competitive market eventually recognize value, it makes sense that this style should perform well over the long term. This is exactly what has played out in practice.

Looking at a long-term history, not only has value outperformed the broader market, it has also outperformed its flashier cousin, growth (see Chart 5.4). The chart tracks the relative performance of US large cap value stocks versus growth stocks. A rising line indicates that value is appreciating faster than growth. As can be seen, over the very long term value has outperformed growth. That said, value has struggled in recent years, indicated by a declining line, as a slow economy has caused investors to favor companies that are more growth-oriented.

Chart 5.4: Russell 1000 Value vs Russell 1000 Growth, 1980–2017

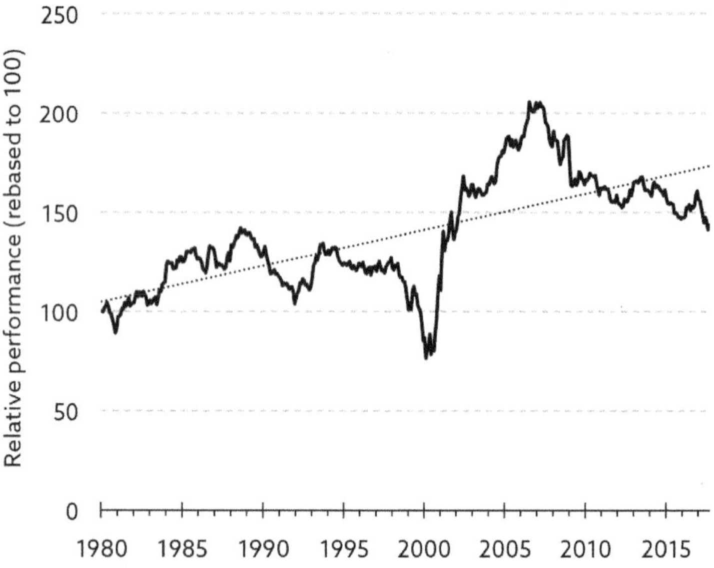

Source: Bloomberg, March 2017.

That said, there are challenges to investing in value. To start, how do you define it? Value can be in the eye of the beholder, and there is no single universally accepted definition of a cheap stock.

Most studies, particularly early ones, have defined value based on price-to-book (P/B). But this doesn't necessarily mean that P/B is the definitive value metric. Instead, the fondness for price-to-book stems from a more basic consideration. P/B tends to be more stable than price-to-earnings (P/E) or price-to-cash flow (P/CF), both of which vary more depending on economic conditions.

Another challenge in building a value exposure is taking into account the tendency for some sectors to be cheaper than others. Bank stocks will almost always appear cheaper than consumer staples companies. If you're not careful, a value fund can load up on the former while ignoring the latter. Doing so would create a portfolio that is dominated by a sector bet, rather than a style one.

This suggests that investors need to be careful when investing in value funds. Whether they gain access through a mutual fund, ETF or try to build their own portfolio, investors need to make sure that they don't disproportionately load up on a particular sector. The best way to avoid this is to measure value within a particular sector, rather than making the apples to oranges comparison of comparing a utility company to a copper miner.

Despite these challenges, value investing makes sense. But that does not mean value is the only factor that investors should tilt towards. Since the end of the financial crisis, a less well known but also powerful style tilt has gained popularity: minimum volatility.

Minimum volatility

The argument for minimum volatility is slightly different than value. While value tends to outperform the market on an absolute basis, minimum volatility is more about risk-adjusted returns. Over the long term, these portfolios have managed to produce returns that are similar to the broader stock market, but with less risk.

Chart 5.5 shows the performance of two popular, global equity ETFs – the iShares All-Country World Index (ACWI) and the iShares All-Country World Index Minimum Volatility – and illustrates how these strategies have performed in recent years. Since 2012, both ETFs have produced nearly identical price returns, 0.64% per month for ACWI and 0.67% per month for ACWI minimum volatility.

Chart 5.5: MSCI ACWI vs ACWI Min. Vol. Strategy, 2012–2017

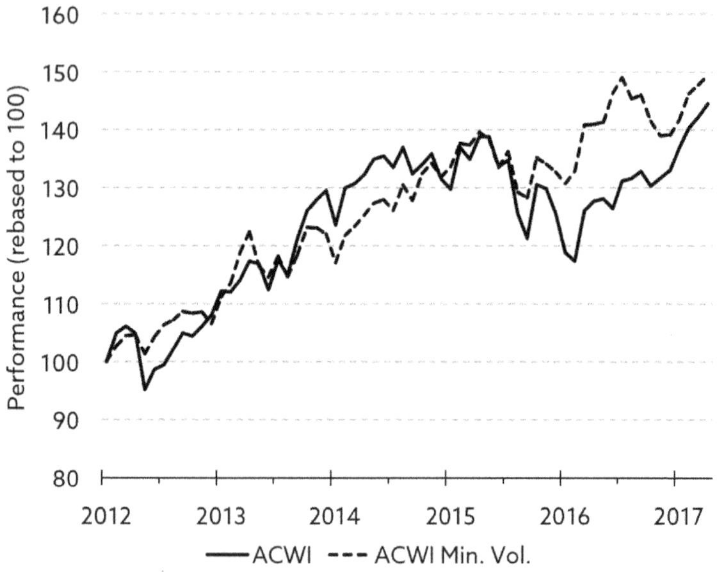

Source: Bloomberg, iShares, April 2017.

The difference between the two ETFs lies in their respective volatility. As the name implies, the minimum volatility ETF delivered those returns with considerably less volatility. During this period the standard deviation of monthly returns was 3.4% for ACWI but only 2.7% for the minimum volatility fund. On an annualized basis this works out to approximately 11.9% for the ACWI and 9.3% for minimum volatility, which is a substantial difference with no loss in return.

When low volatility does not perform as advertised

While minimum volatility tends to produce attractive long-term risk-adjusted returns, there are circumstances when performance is challenged, as with any style. Often this occurs when interest rates are rising. A recent example was the spring of 2013, when markets suddenly became volatile.

Since the financial crisis, most spikes in volatility have been due to recession fears or political uncertainty. However, in this instance there was a different culprit: the Fed.

Back in early 2013 investors reacted violently, and in retrospect prematurely, when Fed officials publicly mused about withdrawing monetary accommodation. After many years of ultra-cheap money investors did not take this particularly well. The subsequent sell-off has come to be affectionately known as the taper tantrum. What was interesting about this instance is that, unlike previous bouts of market dislocations, minimum volatility strategies did not outperform. Arguably the reason was that in this instance, rates went up rather than down.

In May of 2013, during the midst of the taper tantrum, US 10-year Treasury yields spiked from about 1.60% to well above 2%. The sudden jump in yield created a short-lived but sharp rise in volatility. In this instance, the low volatility style performed worse than the broader market (see Chart 5.6).

Why did this particular sell-off cause minimum volatility strategies to struggle? The reason is that many of the stocks favored by this style tend to be more defensive. And as discussed previously, these stocks tend to be owned primarily for their dividends, making them more rate sensitive than other parts of the market. When rates rise, particularly if the rise is rapid, defensive, dividend-paying stocks can suffer disproportionately.

None of the above invalidates the style, but it illustrates an important point. Style factors, like asset classes, can go in and out of fashion. Even styles, such as value, momentum and minimum volatility, all of which make sense over the long term, can still go through periods when they are out of favor and underperform the broader market.

Chart 5.6: ACWI Min. Vol. vs ACWI relative performance, January 2013–September 2013

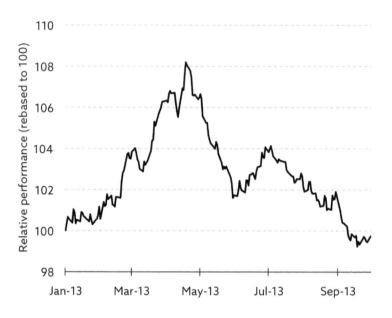

Source: Bloomberg, April 2017.

Why do styles work in the first place?

At this point a skeptical investor might rightly ask why these particular approaches work. It is all well and good that these styles have outperformed in the past, but we've all been conditioned to remember that "past performance is no guarantee of future results." What accounts for certain styles outperforming and, more importantly, is that outperformance likely to continue into the future?

There is a vigorous academic debate over why these particular styles should offer superior long-term returns. The truth is there are competing theories. No single explanation is sufficient to explain the premium investors have received from the various styles. That said, there are a few explanations that are worth considering.

For many, momentum is arguably the most puzzling style. Buying stocks simply on the basis that they're already rising seems strange. By definition, those same stocks will be more expensive, which flies in the face of the value argument. Do you really want to own something simply because others have been chasing it? The short answer is yes, or at least in part of a portfolio.

Momentum has historically produced outsized returns across just about every asset class. As to why this should work, theories abound, most of which are grounded in investor behavior. Human beings do not act rationally in financial matters any more than they do in other endeavors.

One of the best explanation for momentum's success is that investors tend to underreact to news. When there is good news on a stock the initial reaction is less than it should be. As the news slowly permeates the investment community and investors give it proper weight, the security or asset continues to rise. This creates a momentum effect.

What about low volatility? This phenomenon may be even less obvious, particularly when you consider the principle introduced in the beginning of the book: return scales with risk. How can less risky securities produce similar returns to those that are riskier?

There are several potential explanations to the low volatility premium. One is that some investors, particularly institutions, are restricted in what they can do. Large institutional investors, such as pension funds and insurance companies, are often limited in the use of leverage. Unlike individual investors they cannot borrow money to magnify returns.

Rather than borrowing money to juice their returns, some will turn to buying riskier stocks in the hopes of achieving higher returns, which they need to meet their liabilities. By ignoring less risky securities, these large investors leave untouched the low volatility stocks for the rest of us to exploit. This is one explanation on why minimum volatility still offers superior risk-adjusted returns.

Another theory is that low volatility stocks benefit because investors, regardless of constraints, are drawn to more glamorous, growth companies. Like moths to a flame investors favor sexier, story stocks and ignore less volatile securities. Again, by ignoring more boring but often quite profitable businesses, an opportunity is created for investors who are willing to be patient.

The other persistent but somewhat inexplicable factor that has been additive over the long term is value. Many of the world's top investors, most notably Warren Buffett, espouse the doctrine of value. There are reams of academic studies supporting the notion that value works over the long term. If everyone knows value works, the opportunity should have been eliminated decades ago. Why do some segments of the market remain inexplicably cheap?

One very plausible explanation is that it is often far from obvious what is cheap and what is *cheap for a reason*. Assessing value requires making an accurate judgement as to the assets of a company, which is much harder to do in an age when more and more of a company's assets tend to be intellectual or intangible, such as brand. Given this uncertainty, value investors accept more volatility as the price of owning out-of-favor companies. The premium compensates investors for accepting the uncertainty, and often volatility, that accompanies value stocks.

Consider tilts

There is a robust body of academic and empirical evidence to suggest that style investing works. Investors should be aware of these exposures in their portfolios. Value, momentum, quality, size and minimum volatility have all been proven to be additive over time. Investors should consider tilting their portfolio in the direction of some or all of these factors.

This can be accomplished in several ways. Investors can invest with managers that adopt these styles. Increasingly, they can also add these exposures directly to their portfolio through ETFs that are designed to capture these particular tilts.

Key concept: factors as a driver of return

- Factors represent a different way to view a portfolio.
- Macro factors are based on key characteristics of the economy such as economic growth, interest rates or inflation.

➥ Style factors are drivers of return within asset classes. Key style factors include value, momentum, quality and minimum volatility.

➥ Over a multi-decade horizon, certain style factors have produced superior risk-adjusted returns. Investors may want to consider including or tilting their portfolio towards these factors.

Timing factors

Engineering long-term tilts towards certain styles can be a source of incremental return or risk management. Investors could simply substitute a value fund or ETF for part of their equity exposure. Alternatively, they could decide to gain their exposure to a particular region, such as emerging markets, through a minimum volatility approach rather than a traditional index fund.

All of these approaches assume a more-or-less permanent tilt in the direction of a particular style. Another approach, albeit a much harder one, is to time factors, i.e. tactically shift the portfolio in the direction of certain factors or styles based on expectations for the market environment.

Make no mistake, this is not an easy thing to do. Timing factors is no easier than timing markets. But while difficult, investors should at least be aware of the potential to make tactical shifts in their factor exposure as well as the types of forces that typically drive changes in investor preferences.

A good example of when tilting might be advantageous is value. As highlighted above, there has historically been a benefit to adopting a value bias in a portfolio. However, just because value works over the long term, it does not mean it always works. We are currently in a period, a quite prolonged period, when value has been struggling.

Who needs value?

This is not the first time in history, although it is one of the longer stretches during which value has not delivered. During the boom years of the tech bubble many value investors lost faith; growth companies trounced value year after year. The situation became so dire that many money managers tried to convince themselves that tech companies without earnings, revenue or even a cogent business model were *value* stocks. The metrics some resorted to – such as the number of eyeballs looking at a website – would have been funny if things had not ended so badly for so many investors.

Value's underperformance in the late 1990s was driven by an insatiable love affair with a few tech superstars. More recently, value has underperformed for a somewhat different reason. Unlike the late 1990s, today most of the world is stuck in a slow-growth mode.

In a world in which *economic* growth is scarce, investors often favor companies that can generate organic *earnings growth* regardless of the state of the economy. This favors growth companies, particularly those tied to a secular theme, such as online shopping, over value stocks.

In addition, value often comes with volatility. As investors remain understandably traumatized by the last couple of stock market crashes, many have put a premium on safety and consistency. This has supported more defensive, quality companies at the expense of value.

This preference for growth on one hand and safety on the other has left value stocks stuck in the middle. As a result, this style has struggled, particularly as the economy has slowed from the mid-2014 peak. The underperformance of value is evident in Chart 5.7, which measures the performance of the MSCI USA Value Weighted Index versus the S&P 500. The downtrend evident since early 2016 indicates that a portfolio emphasizing large and mid-cap value stocks produced lower returns than the broader stock market.

The weakness of value during early 2016 demonstrates another vulnerability of the style. Not only is value's efficacy somewhat tied to views on growth, but it becomes particularly important when growth concerns lead to market volatility. Generally, value struggles when investors are so worried about growth that worries start to morph into recession fears.

The most recent example of this type of behavior was the period between late December 2015 and mid-January of 2016. During those few months, volatility, as measured by the VIX Index, soared over 100%.

Volatility spiked as investors became increasingly concerned about China, oil and global growth in general. It was also a period in which value underperformed the broader market.

Chart 5.7: MSCI USA Value Factor vs S&P 500, 3 January–11 February 2016

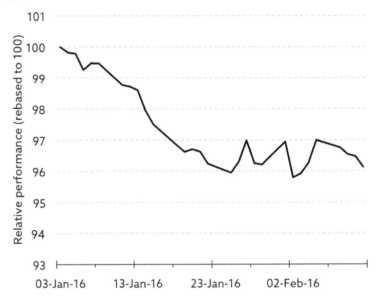

Source: Bloomberg, April 2017.

In one sense this seems counterintuitive. If investors are worried about the stock market, shouldn't they sell their most expensive, overpriced stocks first and hold on to those that represent the best value? Unfortunately, as discussed previously, when investors panic they get short-sighted. During these periods investors want safety, regardless of cost.

Under these circumstances, investors are more likely to hold on to, or even buy more, stocks or other assets that are considered safe. Often these assets are expensive, as investors are willing to pay a premium for the perception of safety. During these periods, the long-term benefits of value are trumped by the short-term aversion to volatility.

The lesson here is that for investors looking to time value, views on the economy and market volatility are key. If an investor is more confident that growth is likely to accelerate, increasing risk appetite in the process, they should consider tilting even more towards value. However, growing concerns about the economy, particularly a recession, argue for some reduction in value exposure.

Size and risk appetite

Another example of a style that can be out of favor for long periods is size. Academics long ago uncovered the fact that even after adjusting for volatility, companies with lower market capitalisations (small caps) tend to outperform. As with value, momentum and minimum volatility, size is a factor that investors should consider tilting towards. However, as with all the other style factors, size does not always work.

While small caps have outperformed large caps over the long term, the strategy has been ineffective for prolonged periods of time. In particular, as with value, small caps underperformed during the tech boom of the mid- to late 1990s. During those years, large cap growth companies dominated other styles.

Chart 5.8 helps illustrate the concept. It looks at the relative return of the Russell 2000 Index of small cap companies versus the large cap S&P 500. The fact that the line rises over the long term confirms that, at least in the United States, small cap stocks have generally produced moderately higher returns. However, as the chart also indicates, there are prolonged periods when that is not the case.

The best example of a period of small cap underperformance was the late 1990s. As some will remember, that was a time dominated by large cap growth companies, particularly tech firms. During that five-year period investors were not particularly interested in small cap companies, value plays or pretty much anything that was not a large cap technology company. However, as large cap valuations reached absurd levels in the late 1990s, investors rediscovered the style.

Chart 5.8: US small caps vs large caps, 1990–2017

Source: Bloomberg, April 2017.

While there are many lenses through which to view the relative performance of small caps, one of the more effective is risk appetite, i.e. are investors behaving aggressively or defensively. There are many ways to measure this behavior. One of the more reliable is to use credit markets as a proxy for investors' appetite for risk.

When credit spreads are compressing, indicating an appetite for riskier bonds, small caps tend to outperform large caps. Conversely, when spreads are widening, suggesting a preference for safer bonds, small caps are more prone to trail less volatile, large-cap companies. Since 1990, monthly changes in high-yield spreads have explained more than 10% of the variation in the monthly relative performance of small cap companies.

Chart 5.9: Small cap relative performance vs credit spreads

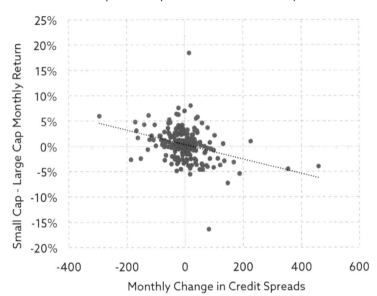

Source: Bloomberg, April 2017.

Chart 5.9 illustrates the relationship. The horizontal axis represents the monthly change in credit spreads. Negative numbers, i.e. contracting spreads, are indicative of *risk-on* periods. The positive numbers are associated with widening spreads, suggesting caution, or *risk-off*. The vertical axis is the monthly difference between returns on the Russell 2000 and S&P 500, small cap and large cap indices respectively.

The fact that the regression line is downward sloping suggests that periods of tightening spreads, i.e. more risk appetite, are generally associated with small caps beating large caps. In periods when spreads are widening – the right-hand side of the graph – small caps tend to perform worse than their larger counterparts.

At this point some may question the validity of a relationship that only explains 10% of the story. This does not sound like a lot of information. Understanding just 10% means that there is still 90% that you don't know. However, this is a relatively strong relationship for financial data. While far from perfect, if the investor had a strong, informed view on the direction of credit markets, at the margin that should impact the tactical view of how much small cap exposure to build into a portfolio.

There is another important takeaway from Chart 5.9: much of the relationship is driven by extreme observations. The most negative observations, indicative of small caps dramatically underperforming large caps, tend to occur when spreads are expanding the fastest. In those months, investors are the most fearful. It is during these periods that the propensity to seek safety will be at its strongest.

At the other extreme, in those months when spreads are collapsing, typical of the immediate aftermath of market bottoms, small caps tend to beat large caps by a wide margin. It is at these times that investors are rediscovering their courage; they are in the mood to buy the riskiest securities that will benefit the most from a rally. It is precisely during these periods that investors turn to smaller companies as a way to leverage their returns.

The significance of extreme observations is not limited to whether to overweight large or small companies. It is indicative of a broader pattern in many financial markets. In many cases, the extremes are where money is made or lost. Many of the relationships that investors tend to rely on work best at extremes. During more mundane periods, having a view on risk may not tell you as much.

Momentum, quality and volatility

This relationship between style performance and risk appetite is also evident in other factors as well. In particular, risk appetite tends to correlate with whether investors favor momentum or quality, i.e. whether they want to chase winners or play it safe.

The relationship is captured in Chart 5.10, which compares changes in volatility, represented on the horizontal axis, to the monthly return to momentum, represented on the vertical axis. The downward sloping line indicates that the relationship between changes in volatility and momentum tends to be negative. When volatility, again measured by the VIX Index, is rising, momentum returns are more likely to be negative than when volatility is falling. This is because investors are less likely to blindly chase yesterday's winners in the midst of a market correction, an event that often entails a change in market leadership. Instead, when volatility is rising, investors typically opt for more defensive companies or really safe assets, such as government bonds.

Chart 5.10: Change in volatility and momentum returns

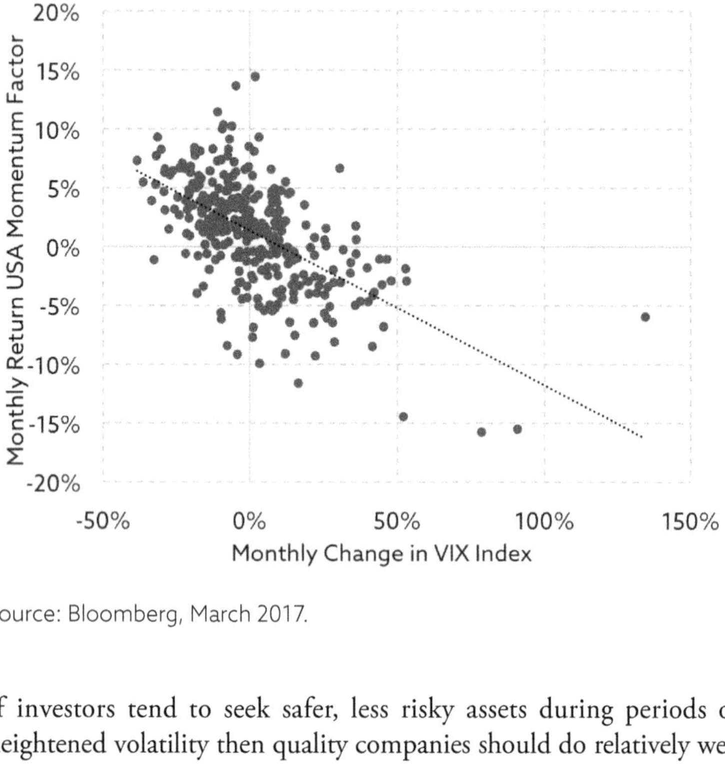

Source: Bloomberg, March 2017.

If investors tend to seek safer, less risky assets during periods of heightened volatility then quality companies should do relatively well in these periods. After all, these are companies that tend to be safer than their counterparts. They are more profitable and generally less risky given lower leverage levels and more consistent earnings growth.

However, when you look at the actual data it appears that quality companies have the exact same relationship that momentum exhibits. Using the MSCI USA Quality Index, we can see that returns to quality also tend to be negatively correlated with changes in volatility (see Chart 5.11).

Chart 5.11: Change in volatility and quality returns

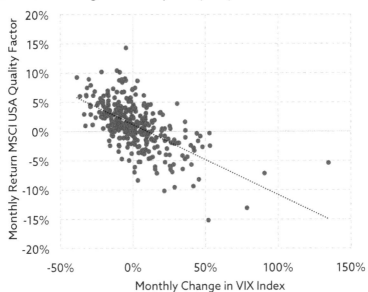

Source: Bloomberg, March 2017.

Why should both styles exhibit the same behavior even though they represent very different investment approaches? The simple answer is that almost all stocks tend to go down when the VIX is rising. Higher volatility, particularly violent spikes, almost always occurs against the backdrop of a market decline. As changes in the broader market tend to drive individual stock returns, regardless of the specific characteristic of each stock, a sharp rise in the VIX is almost always negative for stocks, and negative for all kinds of style factors.

That said, *relative* performance does differ. During periods of market turbulence most stocks go down, but some go down more than others. Riskier small cap and high-momentum stocks tend to be the most vulnerable. At the same time, companies that are perceived to be safer, either due to higher-quality earnings or less exposure to whatever is causing the volatility in the first place, perform better.

Examining the relative performance – the return to quality companies minus the return to companies exhibiting strong momentum – this is exactly the result that comes out. While both momentum and quality companies decline during periods of rising volatility, when volatility is rising quality companies outperform momentum companies.

Where to hide

During the past 25 years, momentum generally outperformed quality under normal market conditions, defined as periods when volatility is falling or gently rising. This outcome is consistent with academic literature which generally suggests that momentum is one of the stronger, if not the strongest, equity style factors.

However, when market conditions turn, the relative performance between momentum and quality tends to shift. When markets are at their most volatile investors develop a laser-like focus on the preservation of capital. At the asset class level this is evidenced by bonds or cash outperforming stocks. Within the equity market, safer companies, i.e. those displaying strong quality attributes, outperform.

This desire for safety over profits is evident in the historical data. As indicated in Chart 5.12, when the VIX is rising sharply, measured as the top 20% of all monthly observations, momentum underperforms quality. In addition, the number of months when momentum outperforms drops from over 60% of the time under normal conditions to around 45% of the time when markets are under severe stress.

The lesson here is that style factors do behave in somewhat consistent ways, depending upon market conditions. If an investor has a strong view on market direction or appetite for risk of other investors, shifting style exposure within a portfolio is a reasonable way to express that view.

Chart 5.12: Monthly relative returns in normal and sharply rising VIX conditions – momentum vs quality

	Average Return	Median Return	Count	% Time Momentum Beats Quality
VIX Normal Conditions	0.34%	0.46%	244	60.66%
VIX Top Quintile	−0.24%	−0.27%	61	45.90%

Source: Bloomberg, May 2017.

Factors and fees: don't overpay for tilts

There is one final takeaway regarding factors. As has been demonstrated, outperforming the market is often a matter of style. When a professional money manager adopts a particular style, whether value, momentum or low volatility, they are more likely to beat the market when that style is in favor. That does not necessarily mean they've gotten smarter, but simply that other investors are more prone to buy the same types of stocks that the manager favors during that period.

If what you're really looking for is more exposure to value, it is not worth overpaying for factor exposure masquerading as skill. Factors are relatively cheap and easy to replicate. If an investor wants exposure to momentum or value, it is not difficult to replicate that style in a portfolio. There is no need for a team of rocket scientists to build a portfolio geared to momentum. All the investor needs to do is purchase one of several liquid ETFs that provide exposure to that particular style.

Given the proliferation of factor funds, investors need to ask themselves the following question when paying the higher fees that come with active management: is the manager really finding unique sources of value or simply performing well when value is in favor? If the former, is it worth paying the higher fees that accompany traditional, active mutual funds? If not, the investor is probably better off in a smart beta fund or ETF. These instruments provide cheap and consistent exposure to most factors through a relatively simple set of rules.

The duality of portfolios

One of the great mysteries of science is the dual nature of light. Numerous experiments in the early 20th century illustrated the paradox. In some instances light is best understood as a stream of particles, known as photons. Other experiments only make sense in the context of light being a wave, similar to sound or an ocean wave.

For years scientists tried to resolve the mystery of the seemingly dual nature of light. Is light a wave or is it a particle? The answer is that light is both. In some contexts it is best described as a particle. Looked at from a different perspective it makes sense to describe light as a wave.

Factor investing and traditional asset classes represent a similar phenomenon. Neither completely describe the picture. Together the two provide a more complete understanding of how to build portfolios.

Factors provide a differentiated view from what you typically get when you think of asset classes. Factors allow you to understand drivers of performance that transcend traditional definitions of stocks or bonds. Low-risk utility stocks, while nominally stocks, are often more influenced by the direction of interest rates than the direction of the stock market. At times, high-yield bonds behave more like stocks than bonds. Factors help to reconcile these seeming contradictions by revealing the underlying drivers of returns – drivers that don't always respect traditional asset class boundaries.

An awareness of factors also highlights the big risk that is often buried in portfolios. Most portfolios have significant exposure to economic growth, which tends to inflict the most pain by its absence. This is true even for portfolios that are well diversified according to traditional asset class definitions. An investor with a big position in a private company or real estate may be diversified by asset class but not by factor. His portfolio is still likely to thrive when the economy is expanding and suffer during a recession or periods of severe investor angst.

Finally, a focus on factors offers the potential for incremental returns. Emphasizing factors such as value and momentum has historically resulted in returns that beat broad market indices.

Successful asset allocation requires multiple lenses. A single focus on traditional definitions of asset classes misses the less obvious, but equally important, drivers of return. Investors need to develop multiple perspectives: viewing their portfolio through the prisms of traditional asset classes, currency exposure and factors. While more abstract than the other categories, factors are no less important.

Key concepts: factor tilting and timing

➥ Investors can engineer long-term portfolio tilts towards style factors that tend to offer a premium.

➥ While tilting to certain long-term factors – notably value, momentum and low volatility – may help improve risk-adjusted returns, factor performance, as with asset classes, is heavily influenced by the economic environment and investor sentiment.

➥ Styles such as small cap or momentum tend to perform best when investors are in a risk-seeking mood. Others, notably quality, perform better on a relative basis when investors are more cautious.

➥ To the extent investors have a view on the market environment, adjusting style exposure is an effective way to reposition a portfolio.

6

Math and Magic:
How to Forecast Returns

THE FOCUS THUS far has been on balancing risk and return. Doing that requires being able to quantify both, or at the very least having some reasonable way to *estimate* each input into the portfolio construction process.

These estimates can be arrived at quantitatively, subjectively or by consulting a psychic. What is not an option is to ignore this part of the process. In order to systematically build a portfolio, these two inputs are needed. Of the two, risk is the easier to estimate.

Risk tends to be more stable. It is safe to assume that the stocks of emerging market companies are going to be more volatile than the stocks of US companies. As a result, most professional investors are comfortable using historical estimates to forecast risk. While not a foolproof method, estimates based on periods from the past provide a reasonably robust method to estimate the risk of both individual securities and broader asset classes.

Return is more difficult. While risk moves around, occasionally violently, returns are even less stable. Returns to any asset class shift dramatically from year to year. As a result, forecasting returns is a humbling exercise. Any forecast will be wrong a good percentage of the time. The key is to be right, at least directionally, a bit more often than a random guess and the rest of the market.

Doing so will require a plan. Investors who succeed in asset allocation are not perfect prognosticators. What differentiates them is a very explicit, deliberate process for forecasting returns. Something that can be measured and refined over time.

If there is one clear takeaway in this chapter it is: *be deliberate*. Have an explicit return forecast. You can change it or even throw it out and start over. What you should never do is ignore it. As you incorporate new information, adjust the forecast but always go back to it. This chapter should help you get a little better in forecasting asset class returns, if only by being more explicit in how you go about the process.

Destination unknown

While central to the asset allocation process, the simple truth is there is no single way to generate a return forecast. Many investors rely on mathematical models, but it is not obvious that these are consistently better than subjective analysis. Still, the investor needs some kind of approach.

A full treatment of forecasting goes beyond the scope of this book, and probably any book, but investors should at least be familiar with their choices. All have their drawbacks. As a general rule, investors should try to favor the simple over the complex, if for no other reason than starting with a simple approach provides a good standard to judge the potential value of adding complexity.

The other key rule of thumb is that investors should think about long-term return assumptions before trying to forecast the next dip or rally. While timing short-term fluctuations in financial markets can be extremely profitable, it is also extremely difficult to see these coming in advance.

Most investors can add considerable value by just starting with the basics: generating reasonable long-term return forecasts to guide a strategic asset allocation. From there assumptions can be tweaked based on valuation, expectations for the economy, or even astrology if so desired. But the first priority is to make sure there is a solid foundation from which to depart.

Don't know much about history

While not necessarily the best or only method, many investors forecast the future by first looking back at the past, i.e. using long-term historical returns. This approach has several advantages, even if you ultimately select a different starting point for yourself.

First and foremost, it is easy and intuitive. Looking at a long enough history provides a rough estimate of what stocks, bonds or gold may return. The math is simple and the approach intuitive. Second, and perhaps most importantly, long-term returns provide a reasonable way to calibrate expectations. This is something that investors occasionally forget.

Recall the earlier example from the mid-1990s. Investors were asked their expectations for the average return on stocks over the next five to ten years. At the time, more than one survey suggested that investors expected annual stock market returns of approximately 20%. Now compare those expectations to what actually happened.

Global equity markets lost more than half their value from the market top in 2000 to the bottom in 2002. It then took about six years to regain the previous peak. During this period, investors had a 0% annual nominal return and a negative return after accounting for inflation. To add insult to injury, soon after regaining their former heights in 2007, stocks plunged again, this time losing roughly 60%. It then took another six years or so to regain the last peak.

To recap, right before the market peak in the late 1990s, many investors expected a decade of 20% annual gains. Instead, investors experienced a lost decade, a period when stocks produced negative nominal returns and even more negative inflation-adjusted returns.

The obvious question is how could investors have been so wrong? What accounted for what, in retrospect, looks like mind-blowing, almost delusional optimism? While it is tempting to dismiss the participants in the survey as ill-informed fools, given the dizzying heights that stocks soared to in the late 1990s investors can be forgiven for their optimism.

While not every global market fared as well, for US investors in the late 1990s, 20% stock market returns seemed like a birthright. The S&P 500 produced total returns in excess of 20% in 1995, 1996, 1997, 1998 and 1999. In 1995 and 1997 total returns exceeded 30% (see Chart 6.1). In this context, a 20% forecast was not particularly aggressive.

Chart 6.1: S&P total return, 1995–99

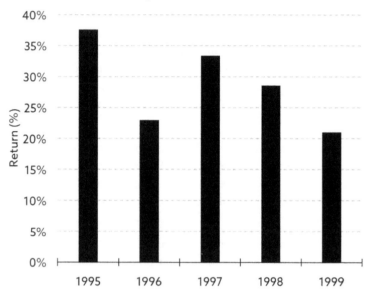

Source: Bloomberg, April 2017.

The mistake people were making was less about euphoria and more about relying on the wrong framing. Investors were putting too much faith in the recent past while ignoring longer-term patterns. Rather than basing their forecast on a relatively short, and as it turned out unusual, five-year period, they would have been better off considering stock returns over a much longer time horizon. Had more people done that, surveys, as well as the market's trajectory, would have probably been very different.

Taking the long view

The benefit of long-term historical returns is that they help frame the possible as well as the likely. In any given period, the economic environment will flatter certain asset classes while providing a headwind for others. During these periods, euphoria will lift those favored asset classes well above any reasonable value, as happened to stocks in the late 1990s.

Unfortunately, these periods rarely last indefinitely. Stocks, gold or real estate – wherever the bull market has been – eventually return to earth. Conversely, bear markets do not last forever either. Stocks rebound, normally at about the time when most investors have thrown in the towel. It is near market tops as well as bottoms that investors are likely to be guilty of excessive optimism or pessimism. Using long-term historical returns helps restore some balance to forecasts.

For these reasons, it is important to be familiar with long-term averages in calibrating return forecasts. If nothing else, long-term averages can serve as a sanity check for whatever numbers you're prognosticating.

Chart 6.2 measures the total return – price appreciation plus any dividends or interest – of the major asset classes during the past 25–30 years. So that you are accustomed to considering risk and return together, the table also provides the annualized risk for each of the major asset classes.

Chart 6.2: Annual return and volatility of major asset classes over different long-term periods

	Annual Price Return	Annualized Risk*	Time Period
S&P 500	11.65%	17.75%	1989–2016
Russell 2000	11.54%	19.26%	1989–2016
MSCI World Developed Countries	6.30%	19.37%	1989–2016
MSCI Emerging Markets	13.84%	34.19%	1999–2016
Barclays Aggregate Index	6.53%	5.05%	1989–2016
Barclays High Yield Index	9.35%	16.23%	1989–2016

	Annual Price Return	Annualized Risk*	Time Period
JP Morgan EM Bond Index	9.38%	10.99%	1998–2016
Bloomberg Commodity Index	4.35%	18.91%	1992–2016
Dow Jones REIT Index	13.94%	18.63%	1991–2016

* Risk measured as annual standard deviation of returns

Source: Bloomberg, MSCI, S&P, Russell, Dow Jones, April 2017.

A cursory look at the above table provides a few hints on how to think about forecasting returns. The first of which is to be skeptical about aggressive return forecasts. A few risky assets, notably emerging markets stocks and REITs, have managed to produce low-teen returns over a prolonged period. This should serve as a general warning to anyone forecasting 20% long-term returns for anything.

As a general rule investors should be thinking about more modest return estimates. As a rule of thumb think about returns in the low-to-mid single digits for bonds, mid-to-high single digits for developed market equities and perhaps low double digits for particularly risky assets, such as emerging market equities.

The second lesson, one we'll return to in greater detail later in the chapter, is that return scales with risk. Not always, and particularly not over short periods of time, but over the long term the potential for high returns comes with high risk. Conversely, safer assets such as bonds should also come with lower return estimates. The risk of an asset should be another consideration when forecasting returns. Indeed, returning to the last chapter, this is the entire premise of the CAPM.

Finally, when looking at returns, even over a multi-decade period, consider the environment. Are the circumstances of the historical period you are looking at likely to be repeated in the future period during which you will be investing? All of the return estimates from Chart 6.2 have a common feature: valuations were rising. In the case of stocks this is captured by the tendency for the P/E ratio to increase over time. The

P/E ratio for the S&P 500 was approximately 12 at the end of 1988. By the middle of 2017 it was 22.

The same pattern holds for bonds. Recall that bond returns are mostly a function of their yield. US 10-year bond yields were close to 9% in late 1988. Today they are barely 2%.

The lesson here is that the factors that drive returns for both stocks and bonds are considerably more challenged today than they were 30 years ago. Any forecast for stocks and bonds for the next ten years should probably be lower than the returns generated over the past 30 years, if only because it is not clear that equity valuations will rise for another three decades, and bond yields cannot decrease by the same amount again (as I explain later in the chapter).

Time of your life

This last point illustrates the main challenge with simply relying on historical returns, even when taken from a relatively long history. It is the same challenge that led investors in the late 1990s to expect a stock market nirvana for the next decade. Even longer-term averages may be unrepresentative if economic conditions change or valuations are at an extreme.

Returning to the question of why investors were so wrong in the 1990s, a simple chart illustrates the problem of relying on any one historical period. An investor living in the United States at the turn of the millennium might be forgiven for her optimism. Not only did the late 1990s produce 20% returns, but so did much of the period that preceded the tech bubble. The stellar bull market of the 1980s meant that even over a period of more than a decade the average return for the S&P 500 was close to 20% (see Chart 6.3).

In this case even a reasonably longer-term average was unlikely to be representative of what was to come. In fact, the exceptional returns of the previous decade were precisely why history was unlikely to repeat itself. Eventually, mean reversion was likely to kick in, meaning that a period of substantially stellar returns was more likely to be followed by a period of sub-par returns.

Chart 6.3: S&P average annual returns, 1989–2000 and 2000–16 (%)

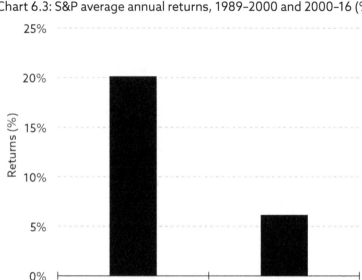

Source: Bloomberg, April 2017.

This illustrates another caveat of relying purely on historical returns. Whenever you see something that looks too good to be true, it probably is. One reason this tends to happen is that sometimes all the stars align in a way that favors a particular asset class. The 1990s was such a period, particularly for stocks. Interest rates fell, inflation decelerated, growth – particularly in the late 1990s – was stellar, and productivity rose.

Unfortunately, these alignments don't last forever. Whenever you see particularly high or low return estimates, ask yourself if the conditions that produced them are sustainable. If not, consider adjusting. As a general rule, if the time period selected is not indicative of future market conditions, return estimates are likely be wide of the mark.

The ups and downs of gold

An even more dramatic example of this pitfall is illustrated by gold. In the 1970s gold was the asset class to beat. Inflation was accelerating and real interest rates were diving deeper into negative territory. Gold typically thrives in this type of an environment. Between 1971 and the end of 1981, gold produced annualized returns of approximately 32% (see Chart 6.4). In 1979 alone the price of gold more than doubled.

Chart 6.4: Gold average annual returns across long-term periods, 1971–2016 (%)

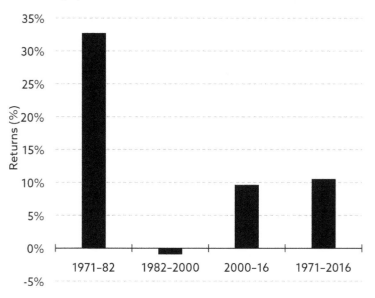

Source: Bloomberg, April 2017.

Now compare those returns with those experienced in the 1980s and 1990s, when the economic environment and Fed policy were very different. Starting in the early 1980s the Fed, under its new Chairman Paul Volcker, took a hard line against inflation. In order to bring down prices the Fed aggressively pushed up short-term rates. By driving up both real and nominal interest rates, the Fed induced a brutal recession. However, by tightening monetary policy the Fed did ultimately succeed in its goal of bringing inflation under control.

As inflation collapsed and real interest rates rose, investors reconsidered the value of gold. Gold tends to be a less attractive investment when real interest rates are high. Under these circumstances, investors tend to sell gold in favor of income-producing assets. Why accept a lump of metal that produces no income when bonds are paying interest 5%–6% above the rate of inflation? It was during this period, lasting roughly two decades, when the annual return to gold was negative.

More recently things have turned again. While nowhere near the heyday of the 1970s, gold returns have been respectable of late. This latest change in gold's prospects reflects the fact that the current environment looks very different from either the stagflation of the 1970s or the low-inflation boom years of the 1990s.

The past 16 years have generally been distinguished by slow growth, low inflation and unusually low interest rates. As discussed in Chapter 1, the latter is at least partly a function of central banks employing evermore creative strategies to create easy monetary conditions.

When low short-term rates proved insufficient, central banks upped their game and expanded their toolkit. Since the financial crisis, the world's central banks have been on a spending spree, buying trillions of dollars of government bonds and in some cases whatever else they could find to purchase.

This has created a unique environment: little inflation but low or often negative real rates. While this environment has not produced the type of stellar returns gold enjoyed in the 1970s, partly because investors have been less concerned about inflation, it has led to a period of sustained, high single-digit returns for gold.

For an investor trying to figure out where we go from here, the question can be framed as follows: going forward, which regime do you expect? If you believe that irresponsible monetary policy from the world's central banks will eventually lead to a bout of inflation, your return expectations should center on the double-digit gains of the 1970s.

Alternatively, if the more recent past is prologue to the future returns are likely to be positive but more muted than those in the 1970s. And what if you don't have a view on what the Fed is going to do or where interest rates are headed? The simplest solution is to use the longest-term data series you can find.

In the above example, the 40-year average produces a result that encompasses the eye-watering returns of the 1970s, the depths of the gold bear market in the 1980s and 1990s, as well as more recent returns. As a result, long-term returns tend to be more muted than shorter-term averages. They also tend to be more stable and, hopefully, realistic. While not the best solution, if you have no view as to what the world is going to look like, the long-term estimate is a reasonable starting point.

When the long term lies

For investors that want to embrace the simplicity of using historical returns, *longer is better* is probably the soundest advice. However, before moving on to other methods, it is worth highlighting instances when even the very long term can be misleading. The bond market probably provides the best illustration of this challenge.

Chart 6.5: US 10-year Treasury yield (%)

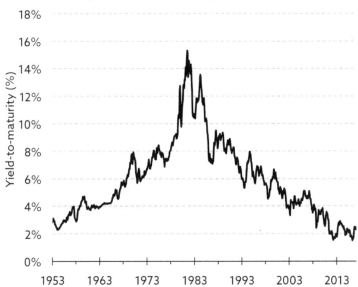

Source: Bloomberg, April 2017.

For the past 36 years, interest rates have been falling around the globe. Long-term rates peaked in the early 1980s. In the United States, the yield on a 10-year Treasury reached more than 15%. From there yields have been on a more-or-less steady decline, culminating during the summer of 2016 when the yield on the 10-year US Treasury hit an all-time low of less than 1.40% (see Chart 6.5).

Falling rates are great for bondholders. As rates fall, other investors are willing to pay a premium for higher-yielding bonds. This causes bond prices to rise. Anybody who has been invested in bonds for the past 36 years has rarely lost money. In fact, the annual total return on the Barclays Aggregate Index, a well-followed index of US bonds, has been negative on only three occasions. From 1978 to 1993 there was never even a single year in which the index produced a negative return (see Chart 6.6).

Chart 6.6: Barclays Aggregate Index annual return, 1978–2016 (%)

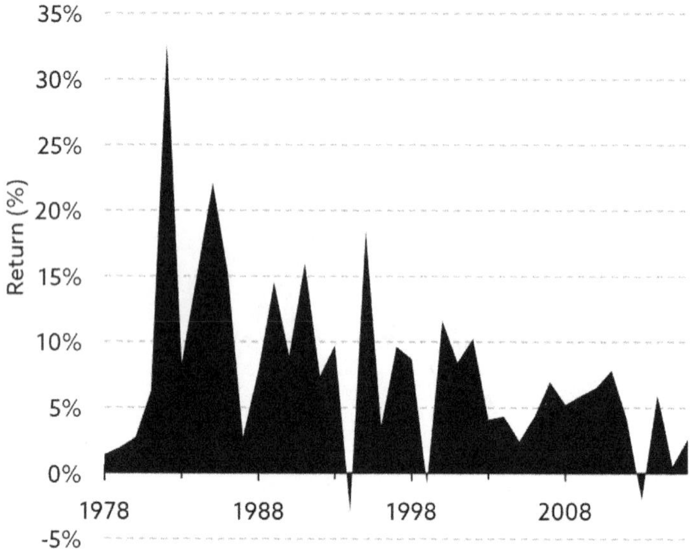

Source: Bloomberg, April 2017.

The persistence and magnitude of the bond market rally has been an invaluable tailwind for portfolios. Bonds were traditionally thought of as the safe, low risk, even boring asset class. You owned bonds for a steady income and a good night's sleep, not to make a killing. Despite this, the average annual total return on the Barclays Index over the past 39 years has been a more than respectable 7.6%. Even more impressive, the asset class has delivered consistent high single-digit returns with very modest volatility.

During this incredible run, the annualized risk of this index has been less than 7%. Any investor that owned a mutual fund or a collection of bonds that mimicked the index received more than a unit of return for every unit of risk. That is rare for a broad asset class, such as bonds, that is liquid and that everyone can easily purchase. It is even rarer that the trend has lasted for as long as it has.

Given this stellar performance, shouldn't everyone just buy a bond index fund and go to sleep? While some investors have higher expectations or needs, for many people a 7%–8% annual return coupled with a smooth ride would be more than satisfactory. Even for investors that want the higher returns that equities promise, the experience of the past 35 years suggests that a good deal of their portfolio should be invested in bonds.

The problem with this line of reasoning is that the factors that drove this multi-generational rally are unrepeatable. At the start of the bond bull market inflation was running in the double digits. The precipitous fall in bond yields that fueled the rally was largely predicated on a successful campaign by central bankers to eradicate inflation. The good news is they won. The bad news is that having won they can't repeat the same trick twice. If anything, today many central bankers fret over too little rather than too much inflation.

With inflation already slain and real rates close to zero, today yields have far less room to fall. This means there is little prospect for capital gains. More importantly, yields, which traditionally provide most of the return, are exceptionally low. During the period when bonds produced +7% returns, ten-year yields averaged approximately 6.3%. A large part of the stellar return to bonds was a function of bondholders simply receiving higher interest payments. This is something that today's bond investor no longer enjoys.

Even relative to the last ten or 20 years, a period when bond yields and inflation were already modest, bond returns are likely to be lower. As recently as 2006, ten-year US yields were above 5%. A bond buyer today is lucky to get half that yield in the United States and an even smaller fraction in Europe or Japan.

The bond example demonstrates why simply relying on past returns can occasionally lead to bad results. Today, the only way an investor could generate a consistent 6% or 7% total return on bonds would be if interest rates fell sharply, eclipsing the all-time lows seen in 2016. While possible, this is unlikely.

Risk and return in the real world

If historical returns are not the answer, or at least not the complete answer, what else should investors consider when trying to forecast returns? Going back to the premise of Chapter 3, investors should cross-check their assumptions of returns against risk. While stocks or bonds can over- or underperform for a period, in the long term returns generally scale with risk. Your return expectations for riskier assets should almost always be higher than your expectations for less risky assets.

The table in Chart 6.2 provided a sample of return assumptions for many of the major asset classes. Included in the table was their realized risk (*realized risk* refers to what actually happens, *ex-ante risk* is what you expect to happen). Chart 6.7 looks at the same data but in graphical form. The point is to illustrate that the returns scale in a linear fashion with risk; the riskier assets have produced higher returns.

Looking Chart 6.7, there are asset classes that look out of place, or instances where returns do not neatly line up with risk. The most glaring example from this data set are the returns to non-US developed countries, notably Europe and Japan. They are substantially below what you'd expect given their riskiness. This is largely due to the long-term underperformance of Japan, which was discussed in Chapter 4.

Commodity returns also appear low relative to what their risk would imply. This should not be a huge surprise given that much of this period was marked by a bear market in commodities. At the same time, US stocks and real estate investment trusts (REITs) produced higher returns than their level of risk would suggest.

Chart 6.7: Major asset class risk and return, 1989–2016

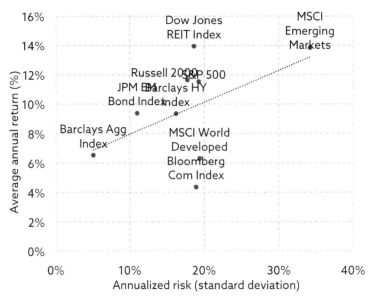

	Risk	Return
S&P 500	17.75%	11.65%
Russell 2000	19.26%	11.54%
MSCI World Developed Countries	19.37%	6.30%
MSCI Emerging Markets	34.19%	13.84%
Barclays Aggregate Index	5.05%	6.53%
Barclays High Yield Index	16.23%	9.35%
JP Morgan EM Bond Index	10.99%	9.38%
Bloomberg Commodity Index	18.91%	4.35%
Dow Jones REIT Index	18.63%	13.94%

Source: Bloomberg, April 2017.

While not a perfectly smooth line, the above chart illustrates that the relationship between returns and risk is not merely an academic theory. Empirically, riskier assets, such as emerging markets, generally produce higher returns than less risky assets, such as government bonds. For anyone looking to forecast returns, risk should serve as the second sanity check.

A little math

As discussed in Chapter 3, there are numerous ways to measure risk, some more intuitive than others. Previously I introduced the notion of a stock's beta as its sensitivity to the market. That concept comes from the CAPM discussed in the previous chapter. In considering the various ways to forecast returns it is worth going into a bit more detail on the theory of the CAPM and its implications for returns.

The CAPM is a long-standing cornerstone of modern portfolio theory. At its core, the CAPM is useful because it provides a simple, or relatively simple, way to relate return to just three factors. Those factors include the risk-free rate (typically the interest paid on short-term government debt), the expected return on the market and beta. The last measure is the most interesting for our purposes. Beta measures sensitivity of a security or asset to the market. Together, these three inputs allow you to calculate the expected return for any security or asset class. The equation for the CAPM is reproduced below in Chart 6.8.

Chart 6.8: Equation for the CAPM

$$\bar{r}_a = r_f + \beta_a(\bar{r}_m - r_f)$$

Where:

r_f = *risk-free rate*

β_a = *beta of the security*

$\bar{r}_m$ = *expected market return*

$(\bar{r}_m - r_f)$ = *equity market premium*

While it looks daunting, the CAPM equation is actually simple, and it is worth getting to know. Stripped of the math, the CAPM simply states that the return to an asset will scale with its riskiness relative to the market. The measure that relates a security or asset class's riskiness relative to the market is expressed as beta.

For anyone who has ever taken a basic statistics course, beta should be a familiar concept. It is analogous to the coefficient in a regression equation that describes how much *y* moves based on changes in *x*. In the context of the CAPM, beta tells you how much return moves as a function of the equity market premium (ERP). Which of course raises the question, what exactly is the *equity market premium*?

The ERP is the marginal amount investors expect to get paid for accepting the risk of stocks rather than embracing the safety of riskless assets. While there is no hard estimate for the ERP, it is generally believed to be about 4%–6%, at least most of the time. Like everything else in finance, the ERP fluctuates. It tends to rise during periods of market stress. During these periods, investors demand a greater premium, in the form of cheaper valuations, in order to accept the risks inherent in stocks. When investors are feeling more confident, the equity risk premium falls as investors are willing to take on lots of risk.

The other key component of the formula is beta. Beta measures risk to a broad market, let's say an index of global equities such as the All Country World Index (ACWI), which is an index that includes stocks in both developed and emerging countries. The more risky segments of the market, such as emerging markets, will have a beta of greater than 1.

Some markets are less risky by nature. In Chapter 2, I mentioned the peculiarities and sector concentration in the Swiss market. The beta of Swiss stocks to the broader global market will tend to be lower than that for more volatile markets. This reflects the more established nature of the Swiss market versus, let's say, China. It also reflects the composition of the Swiss market. A market dominated by relatively safe food and pharmaceutical companies – as Switzerland is – tends to be less risky.

Keeping with the above example, if emerging markets had a beta of 1.6 and Switzerland had a beta of 0.80, you could calculate the expected returns to the stock indices in each of these countries. Assuming an equity risk premium of 5% and a risk-free rate of 1%, this would translate into an expected return of approximately 9% for emerging markets (1% + (1.6 × 5%)) and 5% for Switzerland (1% + (.8 × 5%)). Note that this calculation makes no assumption about the impact of foreign currency exposure.

This calculation illustrates a few key concepts. As discussed repeatedly, stock returns should roughly scale with the riskiness of the stock or index. This is evident in the CAPM, but rather than risk being measured by the standard deviation of returns it is measured by beta.

The second point is that both the level of the risk-free rate and the equity market premium matter for overall returns. Many investors forget about the former. When the risk-free rate is low, as it was in mid-2017, overall market returns are likely to be lower. The reason being that when short-term rates are close to zero, investors will accept a lower return on stocks.

Consider the early 1980s, when stock valuations were still in single digits. One of the reasons stocks were so unloved, indicated by low valuations, was that rates were so high. High interest rates hurt stocks from a number of perspectives, but one of the more obvious is grounded in simple human behaviour. Many investors would be less tempted to accept the risk of a stock if they can earn a high single-digit return on a safe government bond. Higher interest rates make bonds, and sometimes cash, a more competitive investment.

The final and perhaps most important point is that the equity risk premium matters as well. The best time to buy stocks is when the equity risk premium is high. This means investors are receiving a greater compensation for the risk of owning equities. Historically, these periods coincide with times of market distress. Looking at the same issue from the perspective of valuations, when prices are low there is more room for stocks to appreciate. To paraphrase Warren Buffett: you should have the most optimistic return assumptions when investors are panicking and the least optimistic assumptions when investors are euphoric.

Owning the market

One challenge with the above definition of beta is that it is specific to equity markets. What about bonds, cash, commodities and more illiquid types of asset classes, i.e. real estate or hedge funds? For many investors these assets comprise a significant portion of a portfolio. Does the CAPM have anything to say about them?

As it turns out, quite a bit. The mathematics and the logic of the CAPM are not limited to the equity market but apply to all risky assets. The challenge when applying the CAPM to the broader array of asset classes is defining the market portfolio.

In theory, admittedly more complicated to put into practice, the market portfolio would be the portfolio of everything you could own. This would include liquid investments, such as stocks, bonds and cash. It would also include physical assets, such as real estate, commodities and even collectibles. Finally, it would include private investments: private equity and hedge funds.

From there, the process is identical with the only difference being that the return on the market is the return on the broader, theoretical market portfolio while the beta is the beta to that portfolio. As before, the risk-free rate is the starting point.

This broader view is captured in what is known as the security market line (SML). In this idealized world the line tracing the expected returns of the major asset classes is a straight line. The starting point is the risk-free rate. From there the line progresses to the right based on the beta of individual assets, shown on the x-axis. The slope of the line indicates the marginal increase in return an investor can earn for taking on incremental risk. Chart 6.9 provides an illustration of the SML.

To state the obvious, the real world is messier. Chart 6.7 provides a better illustration of how returns generally scale in the real world. Actual returns rarely march in lockstep with risk, nor do they lie obediently on the SML. In the real world the dots representing asset class returns will be arranged more randomly, although they still tend to slope upward and to the right.

That said, while the line will not be a perfect fit for the real world, it does describe the general relationship between risk and return. Returns estimated over a long enough period and with enough asset classes will generally conform to theory: more risk will be associated with more return.

Chart 6.9: Security market line (SML)

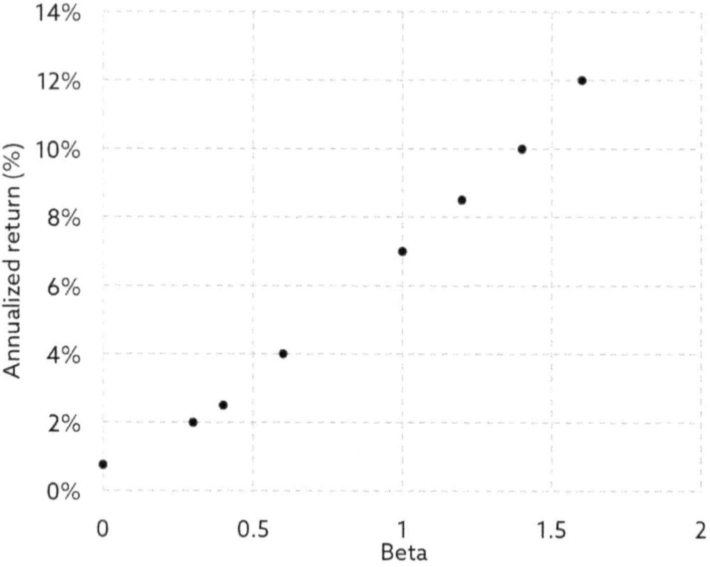

Source: Bloomberg, April 2017.

The practical takeaway is to always cross-check your asset class assumptions against each other. A simple exercise is to plot the expected return against the expected risk. For expected risk, historical standard deviation is a reasonable proxy.

Once you've done this, confirm that the expected returns scale with risk. To the extent that you have a particularly bullish or bearish view on an asset class, the effect should be to push that dot above or below the line. While not perfect, this is a good way to make sure that historical returns, or any other mechanism for generating return assumptions, do not lead you astray.

Key concepts: strategic returns

- There is no single way to forecast returns. Long-term averages are useful, but they can be misleading. Depending on the period used to calculate the average, you can arrive at materially different estimates of long-term asset class returns.
- When using historical returns, always question whether the period they are taken from will be representative of the future environment in which you will be invested.
- Another approach is to calibrate long-term returns based on expected risk. Here, follow a simple rule: return estimates should scale with expected risk, however it is measured.

Value and returns

Thus far the focus has been on long-term returns, but as demonstrated previously market returns can deviate widely from any reasonable long-term average. Stock returns in the years of the 2000s were a pale comparison of the glory years of the late 1990s. Even worse was relying on gold's performance in the 1970s to predict the next two decades.

What causes returns to surge in one period and lag in another? While the list of factors is large, investors looking to refine their return forecasts should start with value.

Value is an elusive concept. You can think about an asset's value relative to its history, fundamentals, or relative to similar assets. For asset allocation the typical comparison is whether or not the asset class is cheap or expensive relative to its history. Depending upon the answer you can further refine your return estimates.

This is easier to do with those asset classes such as stocks, bonds and real estate that produce cash flow, as cash flow can be compared to a price. The higher the cash flow relative to the price, or lower the price relative to the cash flow, the cheaper the asset. In the case of stocks, this is typically represented with a P/E ratio.

While most often applied to individual stocks, P/E ratios are also applicable to broad stock market indices. As a simple example of the relevance of valuation to long-term returns, consider the long-term performance of the S&P 500.

During the past 50 years, the P/E ratio on the S&P 500 has had a discernible impact on the future performance of the index. Broadly speaking, when P/E ratios were above average, returns over the following one, three and five-year periods were considerably lower than when stock valuations started at below-average levels (see Chart 6.10).

Chart 6.10: S&P 500 valuations vs forward returns, 1962–2011

	1-Yr Returns	3-Yr Returns	5-Yr Returns
Below Average	10.54%	36.95%	63.26%
Above Average	5.46%	14.99%	30.76%

Source: Bloomberg, April 2017.

Investors would have done better had they internalized this lesson in the late 1990s. While stocks continued to rise during the 1990s, the premium valuations at the tail end of the bubble led to abysmal stock returns over the five years, starting in 2000.

That said, and in fairness to late 1990s bulls, applying value is never as easy as it seems in retrospect. Investors in the 1990s who sold when stocks first reached above-average valuations felt foolish, and somewhat poorer, for many years. Markets kept trending higher until, for no clear reason, sky-high valuations eventually led to a market top.

Great expectations

The example of the late 1990s encapsulates probably the most common pitfall of relying on value: valuations tell you little about the short term. Value is most useful at longer time frames – with periods of at least a year. As the bull market of the late 1990s illustrates, in the short term prices can continue to deviate from any reasonable valuation for months, quarters and even years.

Even then, while value is probably the best mechanism for adjusting return estimates for longer time horizons, it does not explain everything. It does not even explain most things. Value helps predict long-term returns, but the hard truth is it only explains a relatively small portion of those returns.

Chart 6.10 provided a summation of the impact of value on future returns and it is worth looking at the relationship from a different angle. Rather than averaging all future returns based on the current level of valuations, Chart 6.11 plots all the returns during the same period against the P/E ratio on the S&P 500 one year earlier.

Chart 6.11: S&P 500 valuation vs returns

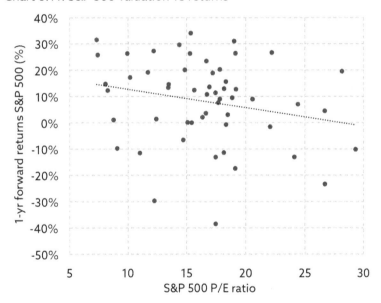

Source: Bloomberg, April 2017.

Chart 6.11 shows that the relationship between P/E ratios and one-year forward returns is negative, as one would expect. More expensive valuations are associated with lower returns during the subsequent year. However, while the slope of the regression line tilts downward, there is a good deal of variation around the line.

Higher values are associated with lower returns, but value explains only a small portion of those future returns. Other things get in the way, leading to many years where returns differ substantially from what value alone would suggest. When it comes to forecasting returns, investors always know less than they would like.

While value does not tell us everything, it is still worth noting. In periods of one year or longer, equity valuations tend to have a meaningful impact on stock returns. Don't let the perfect be the enemy of the good. Value-oriented investors can use value to adjust their return forecasts. Investors should be inclined to raise their estimates of equity returns when valuations are below average and lower their expectations when valuations are at the upper end of their historical range.

Value in bonds: watch the spread

What holds for stocks also holds for other asset classes, or at least those that generate cash flow, such as bonds or real estate. As discussed in the first chapter, bond returns generally follow the interest paid on the bond. This is particularly true for government-issued securities, such as Treasury bonds.

If you want a reasonable estimate of what a bond will return, at least if you hold it to maturity, focus on the yield-to-maturity (YTM). While bond prices will move with interest rates in the intervening years, yield is the best, most robust measure for forecasting bond returns.

YTM is the key metric for government bonds that carry little or no default risk. For other types of bonds – corporate, municipal or emerging market bonds – there is another metric to focus on: *credit spreads*. Here, the basic measure of value is not the absolute level of yield but rather the spread in yield between the asset class and the yield available on a comparable government security.

Narrow spreads suggest that investors are willing to accept a smaller premium relative to safer bonds. Wide spreads occur when investors are risk averse and demand a large premium to hold more risky securities such as high-yield. When spreads are wide it is often the best time to buy high-yield bonds. This is because wide spreads indicate a larger-than-normal premium for accepting the risk of a bond default. When spreads are particularly wide, investors may either be placing too high a probability on default or, as is often the case, are ignoring the fundamentals and are simply selling out of panic. It is at these times that high-yield bonds are cheapest – i.e. they have wide spreads – and often produce the best returns for those with the courage to step in and buy.

As with stocks, credit instruments are cheapest when investors are panicking and shunning any investment that carries risk. Credit will be at its most expensive when investors are the most optimistic. It is during these periods that spreads will be tight, or below their historical average.

For the most part, equity multiples and credit spreads move together, albeit in opposite directions, i.e. credit spreads are tight when equity multiples are at their highest. As can be seen in Chart 6.12 – which shows high-yield spreads for the Barclays High Yield Index – spreads spike during periods of risk aversion, such as after the bursting of the tech bubble and during the 2008 financial crisis. Conversely, calm markets generally witness tight spreads.

When stock multiples rise, investors who owned them at lower valuations benefit. Those who buy cheaply benefit from any subsequent rise in corporate earnings. They also benefit as investors display a greater willingness to pay more for a dollar of earnings. As discussed earlier, this is referred to as multiple expansion.

Consider the change in equity multiples around the financial crisis. In early 2009, investors, traumatized by the financial crisis, were only willing to pay 10x trailing earnings for the S&P 500. Eight years later the S&P 500 index traded at over twice that valuation. Anyone who bought near the lows benefited not only from the dramatic rise in corporate earnings, but also from the fact that eight years later investors were willing to pay twice as much for those earnings.

Chart 6.12: Barclays High Yield Index option-adjusted spread

Source: Bloomberg, April 2017.

Credit markets have a similar dynamic. Instead of market multiples, it is spreads that expand and contract depending on investor sentiment. Assuming a bond does not default, an investor's return is first determined by the interest payments on the bond. But investors can add to their return by buying credit instruments when the spread is wide, in the hope that it will narrow.

The narrowing of the spread occurs as the price rises and the yield drops relative to Treasuries. This is why buying when spreads are wide can lead to higher returns – the investor can benefit from the price of the bond increasing. Conversely, investors risk incurring losses, even after accounting for interest, if they buy bonds when spreads are tight. This is true even if the bond never defaults and investors receive the interest they expected.

This is because widening spreads mean that investors are now demanding a bigger yield premium relative to Treasuries. In order to generate a higher premium, the yield on the bond needs to go up, which means the bond's price goes down.

Just as high and low equity multiples are associated with low and high subsequent returns, spreads drive a similar relationship for credit instruments. Looking at high-yield returns over the past 20 years, the return on high-yield bonds was much higher when investors bought bonds when spreads were well above average. Returns were lower when investors invested in bonds when spreads were tight. This can be seen in Chart 6.13, which shows the correlation between high-yield spreads and forward returns.

Chart 6.13: High-yield spreads vs forward returns

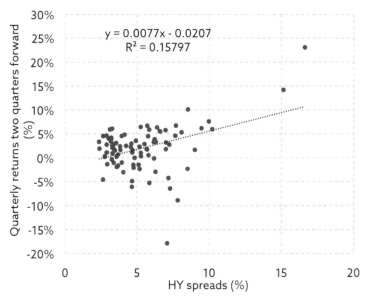

Source: Bloomberg, April 2017.

The relationship between credit spreads and returns is similar to the relationship between stocks and P/E ratios in two important ways: first, value matters most over longer horizons; and second, the value metric leaves more unexplained than explained.

As with equities, high-yield valuations, measured by credit spreads, tell you very little about the near term. In fact, if you look at the relationship between spreads and returns in the very short term, it suggests buying when spreads are actually tight.

Tight spreads do not suggest that investors should overpay but instead reflect one of the factors discussed in the previous chapter: momentum. When spreads are tight, investors are in a risk-seeking mode. This tends to continue for a while. Momentum drives positive returns from trend chasing, at least until the trend reverses. As a result, in the short term momentum is likely to trump value as a driver of returns.

However, value does tend to matter over longer horizons. This is why Chart 6.13 on credit spreads and future returns looks at quarterly returns *two quarters ahead*. Over this time horizon, investors are typically better off buying when spreads are wide, i.e. credit is cheap, and owning less when spreads are tight.

On the second point – valuations leaving more unexplained than explained – the low explanatory power is typical for economic relationships. In economics and finance no single factor explains much. As a result, investors can at best explain a small portion of what drives financial market returns. In statistical parlance, this is evidenced by a low R-squared. In the case of equities, the R-squared is about 5%. In English, this means P/E ratios explain about 5% of the variation in future returns. This means that 95% of what drives future returns is unexplained by this particular value metric.

Not coincidently, credit spreads explain a larger but still modest amount. The R-squared for credit spreads is about 15%, which is better than P/E ratios for equities but still leaving future returns mostly a mystery.

It is not that spreads don't matter. It is just that value, or any other single factor, is always a relatively small part of what influences future returns. Investors can still make money by paying attention to spreads and other value metrics. They just need to have modest expectations about how much they can really predict.

When is value really cheap?

For investors looking for simplicity, you can do far worse than starting with a risk-based return estimate and adjusting for value. As demonstrated above, while you'll still be in the dark about most of what drives returns, this approach provides a sound and intuitive way to adjust long-term return forecasts.

For investors looking to take this process a step further, it is worth asking another question: if valuations and spreads rise and fall, and there is money to be made by anticipating these trends, how do you predict changes in valuations?

Valuations, whether market multiples, real interest rates or credit spreads, are driven by a number of factors, many outside the scope of anyone's ability to predict. Unpredictable events such as the 9/11 terrorist attack or the first Gulf War can have an enormous impact on investor sentiment, particularly if they lead to recessions. As sentiment changes valuations change accordingly.

Under these circumstances, a stock that investors were willing to buy yesterday for 20x earnings may be lucky to fetch 14x. The same holds true for fixed-income. On September 10, 2001 an investor might have been willing to accept a 400 basis point spread on a high-yield bond. When the financial markets re-opened after the tragedy of 9/11, the world seemed much more uncertain. Given these new conditions, investors suddenly demanded a much greater credit premium, i.e. a higher spread to compensate for the uncertainty.

Fortunately, not all market events are driven by exogenous shocks. While terrorist attacks and geopolitical events are impossible to predict ahead of time, there are other, more predictable factors that may provide clues as to the future direction of valuations and returns. By being aware of these factors it is possible to further refine forecasts.

Using stocks as an example, recall that the foundation for valuing stocks is discounting future cash flows. Doing so involves predicting two components: future growth and the discount rate. As the discount rate is in the denominator of the equation, the higher the discount rate, the less the stock should be worth. Put differently, higher rates should equate with lower valuations.

History conforms to theory. Valuations have tended to be higher when interest rates have been lower. Fortunately for asset allocation, this relationship holds at the market level as well as the stock level. Looking back on the past 50 years of equity market valuations, investors have been willing to pay more for stocks when interest rates were low. When rates have been above historical norms, as they were for much of the 1970s and early 1980s, valuations were considerably lower than they are today.

This situation is illustrated in Chart 6.14, which shows the relationship between interest rates and stock valuations, measured here by the price-to-earnings ratio. Historically, equity valuations have been highest when rates were lowest. As interest rates rise, as they did in the 1970s and early 1980s, stocks have tended to trade at lower valuations.

Chart 6.14: S&P 500 P/E vs 10-Year Treasury yields

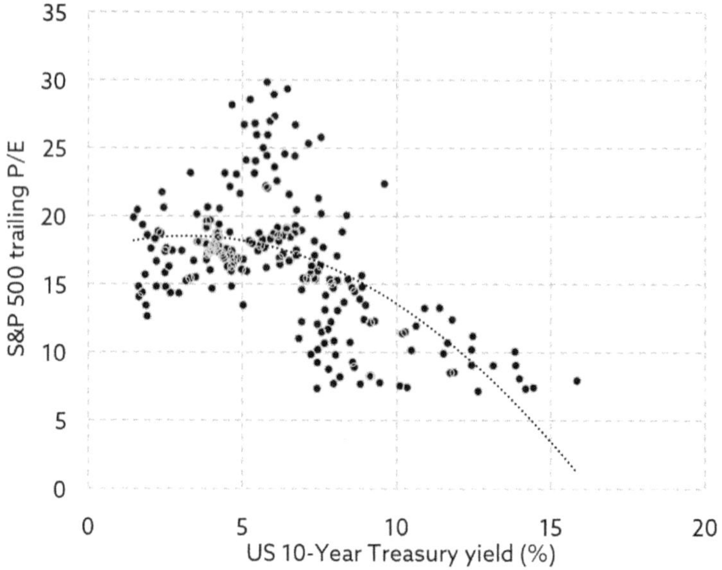

Source: Bloomberg, April 2017.

How is this useful for investors? In trying to answer whether, say, 20x trailing earnings is too much to pay for stocks, take account of the rate environment. While 20x earnings is expensive for most markets, it is arguably more sustainable in an environment in which interest rates are low. In this type of environment, investors are more willing to pay a premium for stocks because bonds don't provide an attractive alternative return.

However, if investors are nervous that interest rates are likely to rise on the back of higher inflation, higher real rates or both, it makes sense to be more concerned about valuations. Under this scenario it would be reasonable to lower expectations for stock market returns, particularly if valuations are already stretched.

Mind the curves

The above relationship – stocks and interest rates – is important for another reason. It raises an interesting question as to how high or low rates need to be. Are higher rates always bad for stocks or does it depend on the level rates are at?

As the previous chart illustrates, valuations tend to go up as rates go down. This conforms to theory and appears to be demonstrated empirically. However, as with the relationship between risk and returns, the real world is never as neat as theory would suggest.

Instead, often these relationships are non-linear, meaning that the level influences the nature of the relationship. In the case of rates and P/E ratios, while P/Es generally go down as rates move higher, the relationship shifts with the level of rates. The impact of rates on valuations is different when rates are very low versus very high.

When interest rates are very low there is not a particularly strong relationship between long-term bond yields and equity market valuations. Whether rates are at 2% or 3%, you would not expect to see much of a change in multiples.

Why should this be the case?

One explanation is that when rates are exceptionally low, as they are today, growth is slow. When growth is slow investors tend to be more worried about another recession than an aggressive central bank. During these periods investors are willing to tolerate moderately higher rates if they are accompanied by faster economic growth.

Historically, the relationship between rates and stock multiples reasserts itself once rates rise above 5%. While there is nothing magical about that number – indeed, many of these seemingly important breakpoints are just the result of random fluctuations in the data – it does illustrate the general concept. Interestingly, the relationship does not seem to change at the other end of the extreme – really high rates.

This asymmetry is driven by the dynamics behind very low or very high interest rates. When rates are extremely low, this is often a sign of a weak economy and investor anxiety. In this context stocks are less likely to be rewarded with a high multiple. On the opposite end of the spectrum, high interest rates, of the type witnessed in the 1970s and early 1980s, are almost always associated with high inflation. Very high inflation is never good for stocks, which is why it is rare to see very high inflation associated with *higher* equity multiples.

Some factors, such as rates, matter more at certain levels. Anyone attempting to forecast returns should ask themselves whether a particular relationship is linear, i.e. tends to be constant regardless of level, or non-linear, whereby it changes depending on the level.

Another example of a non-linear relationship can be found in the high-yield market. Chart 6.13 illustrated the basic relationship between high-yield spreads and high-yield bond returns: when spreads are very low subsequent returns are lower, and when spreads are very wide subsequent returns are above average.

However, as noted, spreads only explain a relatively modest percentage of future returns. Interestingly, they explain more if you allow for the fact that the relationship between spreads and returns may not be linear.

In practice, this translates into reconsidering the relationship in the following light. Extremes in valuation, either very tight or very wide spreads, are the most informative for future returns. In particular, very wide spreads – which tend to happen during periods of panic – drive the relationship.

Chart 6.15: High-yield spreads and forward returns

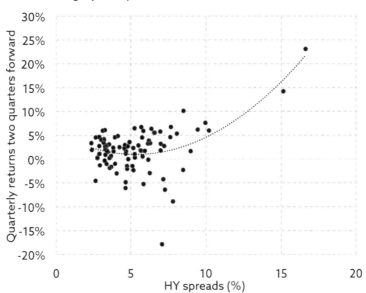

Source: Bloomberg, April 2017.

Chart 6.15 looks at the same data set as Chart 6.13: high-yield bond spreads versus quarterly returns two quarters forward. The time period covered is from 1994 to the third-quarter of 2016. The only difference between Chart 6.13 and Chart 6.15 is the way the relationship is characterized.

The earlier chart looked at the relationship from a linear perspective, hence the straight regression line. In contrast, Chart 6.15 uses a non-linear formula, a quadratic one, to describe the relationship between spreads and subsequent returns. Changing the nature of the model helps explain how spreads really impact future returns.

Leaving aside the math, the important takeaway can be grasped by looking at the scatter-plot. When spreads are close to normal, around 500 basis points, the relationship between spreads and forward returns is not very informative. Yes, there is a slight tendency for wider spreads to be associated with higher future returns, but there are lots of periods when this didn't work.

However, the chart reveals that spreads matter a great deal at the extremes. Using a different type of relationship, one that acknowledges that the relationship between valuation and future returns is not linear, results in a much better fit. In this case, the equation describes about 30% of the variation in future returns, approximately twice the amount in the previous example.

The difference is that the second approach explicitly takes into account the importance of extremes, particularly when spreads are unusually wide. This is really when it is good for an investor to be buying. From an asset allocation perspective, the takeaway is the investor should be most inclined to change high-yield return assumptions when spreads are particularly wide, indicating that the asset class is unusually cheap.

While this does not happen very often – indicated by the fact that there are few dots once you get beyond 8% or 9% on the horizontal axis – when it does occur subsequent returns tend to be very strong. The reason is that these unusually wide spreads tend to happen when investors are truly panicking and markets are close to a bottom. During these periods investors too often ignore value, creating opportunities for those willing to step in and be patient. Just don't expect the same types of returns during less dramatic periods.

Go to the source

By now it should be evident that there are varying methods, of varying degrees of complexity, available for forecasting returns. As will be discussed in the final chapter, before worrying about developing a more nuanced short-term, tactical view most investors would benefit from spending more time on coming up with a robust long-term perspective.

Some will look to improve on those long-term forecasts with a more refined, tactical view – something that takes into account valuation. For investors looking to further refine their value-oriented forecast, they can consider incorporating changes in economic factors and investor sentiment. An even more subtle nuance is to further adjust the forecast based on an understanding of the nature of those economic and sentiment-based relationships.

For investors willing to go to this extreme in trying to improve their forecasts, there is a convenient way to frame the problem. You can break down your return forecast by the sources of return.

For every asset class there are two potential sources of return: the income that asset class generates and the potential for capital appreciation. Income will apply to almost all bonds – with the exception of the type of bond known as *zero coupon*, where all income comes at maturity – as well as dividend-paying stocks and real estate. Income will not be a factor for stocks that don't pay a dividend or commodities.

For the most part, income is easier to calculate. Assuming no cut in the dividend or default by the bond issuer, income is the more reliable of the two return sources. For bonds the coupon payment is typically fixed. For stocks you need to start with the current yield and make an assumption about future growth in the dividends. For the latter, assuming you're looking at a broad market, historical growth rates are again a reasonable starting point.

The second source of return is capital appreciation. Appreciation can occur because the fundamentals change, i.e. stronger earnings for a company or market, or because there is a willingness among investors to pay more for a given earnings stream.

The latter happens when sentiment changes, and investors collectively decide that they're willing to put more of a premium or discount on an asset. Some of the previous examples focused on the P/E ratio for the S&P 500. As demonstrated, how much investors will pay for a dollar of earnings fluctuates over time based on the mood of investors. Over the past 50 years the trailing P/E has been as low as 7 and as high as 30.

In a similar fashion, albeit less dramatic, bond prices also change based on sentiment. Back in the mid-1980s nominal yields were much higher given that many investors were awaiting a return to the inflation of the 1970s. This caused real rates to be high. Yields fell slowly but steadily as those fears ebbed.

Today, after years of low inflation, fewer investors are worried about a resurgence in inflation. Ten-year inflation expectations, embedded in US TIPS pricing, suggest investors expect inflation of less than 2% over the next decade. In Germany, expectations are barely 1%. Over the course of three decades, investor sentiment has shifted in a way that provided a +30-year tailwind for bonds.

Putting these various prices together, an investor can construct a manageable framework to think about the returns for the various asset classes. Start with the income you expect to earn, whether in the form of a coupon payment, dividend or rent. Then consider the factors that drive changes in price. In the case of equities this would include earnings growth and changes in multiples. For bonds it would include changes in interest rates and spreads. The simple sum of these components can provide an approximation of the return you expect for different asset classes.

Forecasting foibles

If readers take nothing more away from this chapter, hopefully the one unavoidable conclusion is that forecasting returns is hard – really hard. There is no agreed upon playbook and every approach has its problems. At best, you can come up with an approximate long-term forecast. With a great deal of effort, and some luck, you may also be able to explain a small percentage of short-term returns.

To further complicate things, market relationships are organic; they are always evolving. Even after you've identified a relationship that makes intuitive sense and has worked in the past, such as interest rates and stock valuations, it may not work in the same way in the future. For example, there was a time when traders anxiously awaited money supply numbers. Today, few pay attention to this indicator.

Factors also rarely work in the same way in all contexts. Value impacts returns, but as the rates example illustrated, often the relationship is most valuable at extremes. The rest of the time value may not provide as reliable an indicator. None of the above suggests throwing up your hands and forgoing the process. Hard as it may be, it is still worth going through the exercise.

The solution for most investors, particularly those with a long-term horizon, is start simple. Use a basic return forecast that appears reasonable, both relative to a very long-term average and the riskiness of the asset class. Then ask if there is anything that might lead to a different result in the future. Extreme high or low valuations are normally the best excuse to change a long-term return forecast.

Beyond that, investors who believe they have skill in forecasting the economic environment, either inflation or growth, can further adjust their forecast. But even here, remember to be cautious. There are lots of moving parts. You might successfully forecast inflation but fail to account for the response of central banks.

And even when investors are right directionally, raising a forecast based on what they perceive to be a cheap asset class, and getting the magnitude of returns correct, is more a matter of luck than skill. Trend followers might have been right to stick with the stock market in the late 1990s, but few would have expected such spectacular gains for so long. Conversely, value investors who expected housing and bank stocks to fall in 2007 probably didn't expect such a violent and disruptive crash. Investors should be humble in their prognostications.

Key concepts: tactical views

➳ Value is a key metric to use in adjusting return forecasts, but investors need to recognize its limitations. The most important of these is that value is most relevant over longer time frames.

➳ Value is also conditional, with *fair value* partly dependent on economic conditions. For example, low rates and low inflation are generally associated with higher equity market valuations.

➳ Many financial relationships are non-linear. They rarely work the same way under all conditions. In many cases, they are most relevant when markets are at extremes.

➳ Whatever changes an investor makes to return forecasts based on more tactical considerations – value, the economy or investor sentiment – in aggregate these will generally explain only a small portion of what happens in the future. Allow for a large margin of error.

7

Some Assembly Required: How to Build Portfolios

THUS FAR ALL of the book has been about assembling the necessary inputs to portfolio construction: a clear objective, explicit constraints, risk, return and a sense of the co-movement of assets. This leaves the final process still somewhat unexplored. How do you take these ingredients and put them together to deliver on investment goals? This process is formally known as portfolio construction.

Before getting to the unavoidable math, it is worth outlining what it is that portfolio construction actually accomplishes. Regardless of the particular method or tools, portfolio construction is designed to produce an *efficient* portfolio. In this context, efficiency is defined as the portfolio with the highest expected return for a given level of risk, or the least risk for a given level of return. Regardless of whether the investor is looking to minimize risk or maximize return, the finished portfolio should maximize the return available for the risk they are willing to take.

In this context there are always trade-offs. An investor could decide that they're willing to take a bit more risk in order to gain incremental returns. A more risk-averse investor might ask how much they can reduce volatility if they were to accept a lower return target. The goal of the portfolio construction process is to make these trade-offs explicit.

Some of these trade-offs won't always be obvious. Am I a 5% volatility kind of investor, or can I withstand 8% volatility? Few of us would find that an easy question to answer. In order to make it a bit easier, one concept introduced later in the chapter is the notion of a benchmark or strategic portfolio. This exercise is useful in translating risk to a rough approximation of what that risk would look like in a real-life portfolio.

The strategic portfolio

The financial ruler: the Sharpe Ratio

Investors can build an infinite variety of portfolios, each with different risk and return characteristics. Comparing an aggressive portfolio to a more conservative one is an apples-to-oranges comparison. They have different objectives. One is focused on preserving capital while the other on producing high returns.

Even if you're faced with a less stark choice, it is not always obvious which portfolio is superior. From the discussion in Chapters 2 and 3, an investor might be able to eliminate some of the choices to the extent they don't conform to her investment goals, or fail to respect key constraints.

That still leaves a lot of possibilities. For example, there are many ways to build a portfolio with a 9% target risk. Assuming they all respect the investor's constraints, which is the right one? Which is better?

While this seems like a question without an answer, there is actually a simple way to compare any two portfolios: the Sharpe Ratio. This is a relatively simple formula for comparing two portfolios, or even two investments, based on the expected return, risk and risk-free rate of return. The goal is to quantify the investment with the best return/risk trade-off. As a practical matter, a portfolio level Sharpe Ratio above 0.50 is a reasonably good outcome.

The Sharpe Ratio is named after Nobel laureate William F. Sharpe. The numerator of the ratio is the return on an investment minus the risk-free rate. The denominator of the ratio is the risk, measured by the standard deviation of returns.

The logic of first subtracting the risk-free rate from the return is that you should not reward a risky investment for the portion of the return coming from the risk-free rate. Today, given that short-term interest rates are still at or close to zero in the US, Europe and Japan, the return divided by risk gives a decent approximation of the Sharpe Ratio.

The significance of the Sharpe Ratio is that it lets the investor compare two investments, portfolios or asset allocation strategies with very different risk characteristics. It reduces the challenge to a simple question: what asset or combination of assets gives the highest return per unit of risk? Once that is known, the investor can focus on the portfolio that is most in line with their objectives and risk tolerance.

Assembling the ingredients

With the Sharpe Ratio as a financial compass we can turn to the question of how to combine return and risk estimates into a portfolio. As described in Chapter 2, the first step in building a portfolio is deciding on the investor's objective. Portfolio construction is at its root an optimization problem. You provide a set of inputs: expected return, expected risk and the covariance of the various asset classes. Then you try to solve for the objective.

The objective could be the combination of assets with the least risk, highest return or something more complicated. As an illustration, it is worth taking a look at what the first two portfolios – minimum risk and maximum return – look like. If nothing else it will hopefully illustrate why asset allocators normally go for something slightly more complicated.

Using the return and risk assumptions in Chart 7.1, along with a covariance matrix that measures the correlation of the various asset classes over a two-year period (June 2014 to July 2016), we can build a variety of portfolios. To be clear, there is nothing magical about the period selected to calculate the covariance matrix. It simply provides a reasonable approximation of recent market conditions, with the implicit assumption that market conditions in the near-term will resemble those from the recent past.

Chart 7.1: Return, risk and correlation estimates

	S&P 500	European equities	Japanese equities	EM equities	US Treasuries
S&P 500	1.000				
European equities	0.849	1.000			
Japanese equities	0.700	0.686	1.000		
EM equities	0.804	0.811	0.633	1.000	
US Treasuries	-0.363	-0.302	-0.387	-0.222	1.000
Non-US government bonds	-0.197	-0.016	-0.383	-0.044	0.587
Investment-grade bonds	-0.005	0.006	-0.140	0.100	0.792
High-yield bonds	0.682	0.645	0.433	0.637	-0.271
US Inflation Protected Securities (TIPS)	-0.049	-0.011	-0.189	0.131	0.784
Gold	-0.242	-0.122	-0.359	0.007	0.445
EM $ denominated debt	0.588	0.601	0.388	0.718	0.066
Cash	-0.043	-0.053	-0.046	0.011	0.149

Asset Class	Forecasted Risk	Forecasted Returns
S&P 500	13.50%	5.70%
European equities	17.10%	6.00%
Japanese equities	17.50%	6.45%
EM equities	21.10%	7.30%
U.S. Treasuries	3.30%	-0.35%
Non-U.S. government bonds	8.90%	-0.05%
Investment-grade bonds	5.20%	1.23%
High-yield bonds	8.20%	3.65%
U.S. Inflation Protected Securities (TIPS)	5.30%	1.40%
Gold	15.20%	0.35%
EM $ denominated debt	7.10%	3.00%
Cash	0.60%	1.20%

Non-US government bonds	Investment-grade bonds	High-yield bonds	US TIPS	Gold	EM $ denominated debt	Cash

1.000						
0.485	1.000					
-0.112	0.196	1.000				
0.568	0.801	0.072	1.000			
0.540	0.337	-0.018	0.422	1.000		
0.106	0.414	0.725	0.378	0.139	1.000	
0.089	0.167	0.024	0.087	0.322	0.104	1.000

Taking the various inputs and combining them is the job of the optimizer. As with the statistical metrics first discussed in Chapter 3, optimization problems are not unique to finance but represent an entire field of study. Optimization routines are relevant to many industries, whether trying to find the most efficient shipping route or the best way to configure a manufacturing process. While the math can assume various layers of complexity, the basic goal is to maximize or minimize some solution subject to various constraints.

For the purposes of portfolio construction, we can reduce this body of knowledge to a particular financial tool: mean-variance optimization (MVO). To be clear, there are other methods for optimizing portfolios. Many of these go by esoteric and somewhat intimidating names: multi-period mean-variance optimization, Black-Litterman and semi-variance, to name but a few. MVO is just one method among many for building a portfolio.

While MVO is not the only way to optimize a portfolio, it is probably the most straightforward. It relies on the ingredients we've already highlighted: expected returns, expected risk and the covariance of the assets. In addition to simplicity, MVO offers several other advantages: there is a long and well-established body of knowledge surrounding MVO and there are a number of off-the-shelf software packages and add-ins that allow investors to use this tool without writing their own code. For example, for those readers who have access to a Bloomberg terminal, there is a simple Excel add-in that allows users to perform an MVO using ETFs representing the major asset classes. The user can use either historical return estimates or enter their own.

Garbage in, garbage out

But before tackling what an optimization can do, it is worth highlighting its limitations. Regardless of the exact model, portfolio optimization is no more than an algorithm, i.e. a step-by-step process for solving a problem. Like most computer programs, it only knows what you tell it. An optimization will not assess whether your inputs are sensible.

If you assume that you can generate 20% returns on the stock market, the optimizer will simply take those numbers as gospel and return you a portfolio with a whole lot of stocks. There is also nothing in the optimization process that will protect you from yourself. If you overestimate your risk tolerance and set a risk target of 15%, that is what the optimizer will use to target risk. If it later turns out that the portfolio is far too volatile, it is not the optimizer's fault. The process simply produced a portfolio based on your specifications.

It is also worth remembering that both return and risk are only estimates. As discussed, the riskiness of assets changes with market conditions. As sometimes happens, normally safe assets, such as government bonds, can become very risky under certain conditions. As both risk and return are estimates, the optimal portfolio is never the optimal in real life. Still, it is the best available starting point.

The efficient frontier

At its core, MVO is basically a calculus problem. Within the context of portfolio construction, the goal is to find the best portfolio based on the investor's objective function, i.e. the goal, and subject to various constraints, such as the amount the investor is willing to hold in any given asset.

For some the natural response is: couldn't I just do this in my head? The short answer is probably not. Remember, it is not enough to enumerate the expected return and risk of each asset. You also need to understand how they co-move.

Even for a relatively small number of asset classes, say a dozen, this is a daunting challenge. If, like most of us, you can't keep a 12 column by 12 row matrix in your head, you should consider using MVO. For those who can do that, your skills may be wasted in asset allocation; card counting or poker may be a quicker path to retirement.

What the optimizer really allows you to do is to take the various inputs and find the most efficient portfolio, being defined as the portfolio with the highest expected return for a given level of risk. A graph of all of these efficient portfolios defines what is known as the *efficient frontier*. This represents the set of portfolios that produce the highest return for various risk targets. What distinguishes an individual investor's efficient portfolio is the one that corresponds to the investor's target risk level.

As Chart 7.2 illustrates, a portfolio representing a combination of assets will always dominate an individual asset. Put differently, there is no single asset likely to produce a better risk-adjusted return. What investors are trying to do is find the best combination of assets, so that the resulting portfolio also lines up with their target risk.

Chart 7.2: The efficient frontier

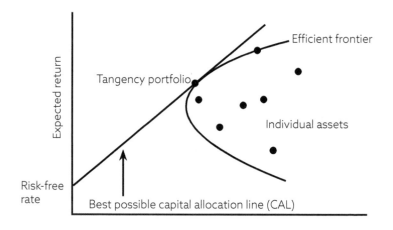

The absolute minimum

What if you had the simplest of goals: be invested in the market but minimize risk. While not advisable, for reasons that will become clear in a moment, the minimum risk portfolio is a useful place to start. If nothing else, this portfolio helps illustrate the pitfalls of focusing on either risk or return without the other.

As the name implies, the minimum risk portfolio is simply the portfolio corresponding to the lowest *expected* risk. What do I mean by expected? Simply that the process looks to minimize the risk of the portfolio based on the inputs you provide. In other words, if all the asset classes turn out to be exactly as risky as you expect, the optimizer will return the portfolio with the lowest possible risk.

In terms of the actual calculations, a minimum variance portfolio is actually simple to calculate, although admittedly not so simple that you can do it yourself with a pencil and paper. In effect, it is a big calculus problem. The optimizer is trying to find the combination of weights for each asset that produces the portfolio with the lowest expected standard deviation or variance.

What is distinct about this portfolio is that the simple goal, find the least risky portfolio, means that the process ignores the return of the assets. The net result is a portfolio that is, by design, very, very conservative. The portfolio is shown in Chart 7.3.

Chart 7.3: Minimum risk portfolio

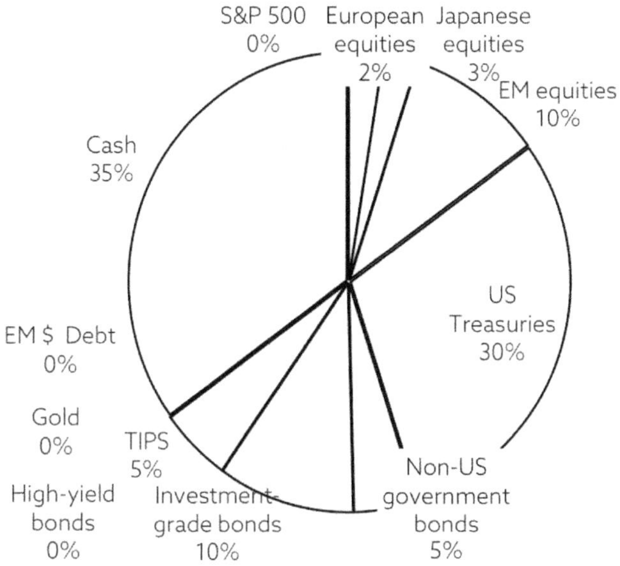

Source: Bloomberg, April 2017.

The first thing to note about the minimum risk portfolio is that it is very timid. Expected risk is just above 3%. This is a portfolio that will let you sleep at night. Unfortunately, it won't do much else.

As returns were not taken into account, the portfolio does not offer much opportunity to actually make money. 70% of the portfolio is invested in relatively safe Treasuries, including TIPS, and cash. The portfolio dedicates only 15% of its allocation to stocks.

As a result, the expected return on this portfolio is low, around 2.3%. This is a portfolio for an individual with a maniacal focus on capital preservation and a relative indifference to returns. Given the lack of stocks or other assets that might appreciate in value, this portfolio will not produce an adequate return for most investors.

Not the obvious solution

While the minimum risk portfolio is clearly not much of a money maker, it is nevertheless worth examining. For starters, despite the objective of minimizing risk, the portfolio is not all cash. The reason is that over the period when the covariance matrix was calculated, US Treasuries had a negative correlation with many asset classes. As a result, while Treasuries are more volatile than cash, they nevertheless receive a significant allocation. As illustrated in Chapters 3 and 4, combining assets that are negatively correlated lowers overall portfolio risk.

Apart from the fact that it is not an all-cash portfolio, perhaps an even bigger surprise is the inclusion of EM equities. Not only did this very volatile asset class make the cut, but of the 15% of the portfolio in equities, two-thirds is in EM stocks.

The inclusion of EM stocks seems counterintuitive. Emerging market equities have historically been more volatile than US equities. They have also been more volatile than other non-US stock markets, such as Europe or Japan. The additional volatility is a function of the foreign exchange risk and the fact that these markets are less developed, and therefore entail more risk. Why would a minimum risk portfolio favor this asset class?

The reason is, once again, correlation. While emerging market stocks are still fairly well correlated with other stock markets, they are less correlated with the United States than European equities. They also have a tendency to move in the opposite direction to many other asset classes, notably bonds. As with Treasuries, by including a modest allocation to a less correlated asset class, even a fairly volatile one, you still arrive at a more balanced portfolio.

Going for broke

If the previous example was all about managing risk, what happens when you throw caution to the wind and try to maximize return instead? In many respects you get the exact opposite of the previous portfolio. The allocation displayed in Chart 7.4 is a portfolio designed to maximize return regardless of risk.

Whereas the previous example had low expected return and risk – 2.3% and 3.3% respectively – the next portfolio is supercharged. The expected return is 6.5%. While that might not seem like a particularly impressive return, remember that the expected return is simply a function of the inputs. We've assumed modest returns given where we are in the market cycle.

If you had more aggressive return expectations you would get a higher overall portfolio return. Despite the modest absolute level, what this exercise produced was the portfolio likely to deliver the maximum return given the return expectations provided.

The higher return, a marginal 4% over the first example, comes with a significantly higher risk budget. Whereas the first portfolio was expected to have an annual standard deviation of around 3%, the second portfolio is expected to have annual risk of over 16%. This is not a portfolio for the faint of heart.

That marginal risk comes via a very different asset allocation. The first portfolio had a scant 15% in stocks. In contrast, the portfolio designed to maximize returns has no cash or bonds. It is all about stocks, with a healthy dose of more volatile markets such as Japan and emerging markets. Collectively these two markets constitute 60% of the overall portfolio.

While the portfolio is aggressive, it is not suicidal. It sort of makes sense in the context of the very limited goal. That said, an investor can do better. By considering risk as well, and not just return, an investor should be able to generate a portfolio with similar return but significantly less risk.

This potential to do better is evident when you consider the portfolio's poor Sharpe Ratio. The maximum return portfolio has a Sharpe Ratio of 0.37, well below the 0.55 of the minimum risk portfolio. While the goal of maximizing returns will almost certainly lead to a lower Sharpe Ratio, an investor can improve on this. What is needed is a more balanced expression of a risky portfolio.

Chart 7.4: Maximum return portfolio

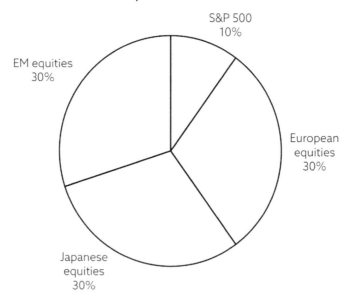

Source: Bloomberg, April 2017.

Taking into account both risk and return

The way to a more robust portfolio is balancing both risk and return, so using the Sharpe Ratio represents the logical next step. The next example explicitly focuses on maximizing the Sharpe Ratio. The result is a portfolio that is somewhat more diversified than either of the previous two examples.

The new portfolio is not all about equities. Nor is it all safe government bonds. There is a mix of the major asset classes. As a direct result, the Sharpe Ratio is a fairly impressive 0.61, the highest of any of the portfolios sampled so far (see Chart 7.5).

Chart 7.5: Maximum Sharpe Ratio portfolio

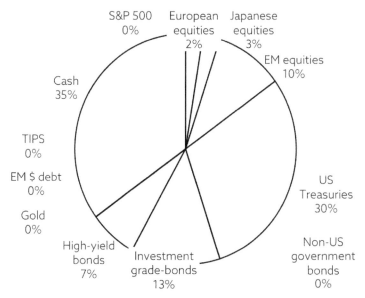

Source: Bloomberg, April 2017.

Is this the best we can do?

Probably not. While this is an improvement over either of the two previous portfolios, there is room for further improvement. The above portfolio is efficient, but boring. The expected return is still quite low, at 2.60%. This is barely above the 2.3% in the minimum risk portfolio.

One of the big problems is that the portfolio contains a lot of cash, arguably too much. The focus on cash is one of the drawbacks of trying to maximize the Sharpe Ratio. Given the low volatility of cash, it is an asset class with a high Sharpe Ratio. However, in the current environment it is also an asset class with little return.

Generally speaking, low-risk assets will have high expected Sharpe Ratios. A portfolio explicitly designed to maximize return versus risk (i.e. maximise Sharpe Ratio) will tend to favor safe assets, notably government bonds and cash. It will tend to be light on risky assets, such as stocks and commodities. This is fine for a conservative investor who places a premium on a smooth ride. It will be less useful for a 30-year-old looking to save for retirement or fund a child's college education.

Stretching your budget

If none of the above approaches are likely to lead to a workable portfolio, how should investors approach the process of portfolio construction? If the goal is balance, the key is to find a portfolio that maximizes return within a particular risk budget. This suggests targeting either a particular return, while minimizing risk, or maximizing return within a particular risk budget.

The next example is based on an optimization targeting return while targeting 9% risk. The 9% risk target is not a random number. This 9% roughly translates into the risk that comes from a classic 60/40 stock/bond portfolio (see Chart 7.6).

This resulting portfolio's expected return is nearly 5%. This produces a Sharpe Ratio of approximately 0.50. While this is well below the minimum risk and maximum Sharpe Ratio portfolios, it is reasonable. As a general rule, any Sharpe Ratio around 0.50 suggests a decent balance of risk and return.

While the portfolio in Chart 7.6 has roughly the same risk as a typical 60/40 portfolio, it differs in a few important respects. The portfolio contains only about 50% stocks, roughly 10% less than a classic allocation. However, the stocks it does own tend to be riskier, including a large allocation to both Japan and emerging markets. Given the return expectations included in Chart 7.1, the process suggests that it is more efficient to hold less stocks but allocate a greater portion of the equity allocation to the riskier segments of the market.

The other way the portfolio makes up for the modest reduction in equity holdings is to allocate to riskier segments of the bond market, including 7% to high-yield and 5% to emerging market bonds. As discussed earlier, high-yield can be thought of as a *low beta* or less risky form of equity. While technically a bond, it behaves very differently than typical government bonds and also offers the potential for higher returns. Other asset classes, such as preferred stock, have similar characteristics and can be very useful for moderate risk portfolios.

Chart 7.6: Maximum return at 9% risk

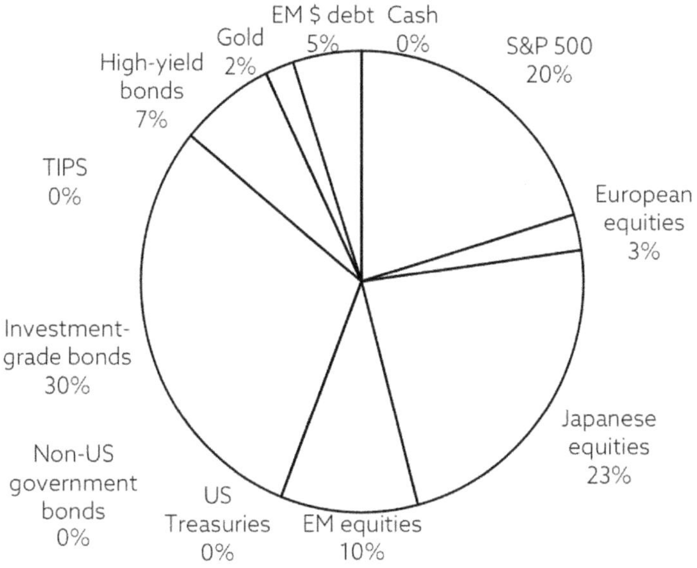

Source: Bloomberg, April 2017.

The rest of the bond portion of the portfolio is comprised mostly of investment-grade debt, with a modest allocation to emerging market debt. Note, there is no government debt in the portfolio. This may be a bit risky, and an investor might want to rethink this allocation. The lack of government bonds arguably reflects the better yield prospects available on corporate debt.

The final point to note is the 2% allocation to gold. While not a particularly large allocation, it is worth highlighting that the allocation occurs despite a near zero expected return. As discussed in previous chapters, gold's value is not in its return but in its diversification properties.

Most allocations seeking to maximize return while minimizing risk will contain some gold allocation, typically around 2% to 5%. This can vary over time depending on economic considerations and the extent that gold is negatively correlated with other asset classes. As a general rule, unless you're in an environment of quickly rising real interest rates, a modest amount of gold can help to diversify a portfolio.

Targeting return

The final example provides a similar approach and result, but starts from the opposite perspective. Here the goal is to hit a particular return target, in this case 5%, with as little risk as possible. The difference between this approach and the previous one is that the metric being targeted in the optimization has been reversed. In the previous example the goal was to maximize return with a risk cap, but in this instance the goal is to minimize risk with a return target.

Chart 7.7: Minimum risk at 5% return

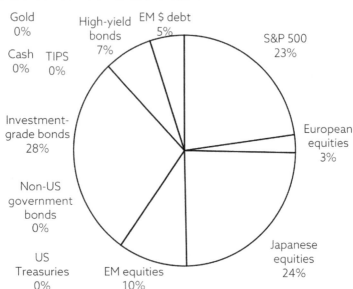

Source: Bloomberg, April 2017.

While the approach is the inverse of the last exercise the results are very similar. This is not a coincidence. In both cases the solution is a portfolio with roughly a 5% expected return, 9% expected risk and a Sharpe Ratio of around 0.50 (see Chart 7.7).

Relative to the previous portfolio, the major difference is a slightly higher equity weight, a marginally smaller position in investment-grade bonds and the lack of the gold position. This is basically a slightly riskier portfolio – 9.6% total risk versus 9% in the previous example. If an investor wanted to lower the expected return to the same as the previous example, 4.84%, the portfolios would be the same.

The strategic portfolio

The last two portfolios could be thought of as strategic portfolios. These are potential long-term allocations that line up with a typical risk target. Investors may decide to shift the allocation from time to time, depending upon changes in their market views, but this is the portfolio you come back to when you don't have any strong views on markets.

While this might seem a bit simplistic, it is a useful starting point. Think of the strategic portfolio as the portfolio best suited to the investor's needs over the long term. It provides a baseline allocation consistent with investment goals. This is the portfolio the investor is trying to beat when they decide to get fancy and time the market. If the investor finds that they can't really time the various asset classes to produce better results, these strategic portfolios are the default to revert to.

Key concepts: strategic portfolio

- ➻ Basic portfolio construction requires two inputs: return forecasts and a covariance matrix.

- ➻ These components are combined using an optimization routine. The traditional approach is a mean-variance optimization.

- ➻ Optimizations can have different goals. Investors should consider a simple construct: maximizing returns subject to a target risk while taking into account any portfolio constraints.

➤ The output of the initial portfolio construction exercise should be a *strategic* portfolio based on long-term returns. This is the portfolio the investor holds in the absence of tactical views.

Tactical views: risk and return

If the strategic portfolio is the investor's starting point, tactical asset allocation (TAA) is the next logical step. Tactical asset allocation is reserved for those investors who feel that they have skill in timing markets. The goal is to incorporate shorter-term, tactical views in order to improve on the strategic portfolio, either by adding return or reducing risk.

Tactical views are adjustments to one or more of the inputs previously discussed: return, risk or the co-movement of assets. Admittedly, when most investors talk about tactical asset allocation they typically think in terms of a different view of returns. However, there are other ways to influence asset allocation beyond changing return estimates.

A view that an asset is likely to be more or less risky than its recent history can also impact the allocation. For example, even without a change in return assumptions, a view that stock/bond correlations were going to rise dramatically would lead to a portfolio of fewer bonds. Differentiated views on risk or even correlations can be just as powerful as views on return.

How then should investors think about the impact of changing tactical views? As a general rule, higher return estimates will raise an allocation while lower returns will obviously have the opposite impact. Changes to risk estimates work in the opposite direction. Higher risk suggests a lower allocation to an asset class, even if it is believed that the expected return remains the same.

At first glance that seems like a strange statement. Does it make any sense to separate views on risk from views on return? If a particular asset class is thought to be riskier, wouldn't that by definition imply that returns will also be lower?

Let's look at this in more detail.

Separating risk and return

Going back to our definition of risk, it is indeed possible for risk and return to move in opposite directions. While this might not make sense given the everyday definition of risk, i.e. something bad happens, it makes sense given our portfolio-oriented definition of risk. In understanding why, it is worth recalling the definition of risk – namely, the variance or the standard deviation of returns.

Unlike other measures of risk, the standard deviation quantifies the breadth of outcomes. It doesn't necessarily tell you anything about the most likely outcome. A wider distribution of returns can include positive surprises as well as negative ones. In fact, market participants often talk about *positive surprises* or *right-tail events*.

Take the following example. Imagine an asset class, let's say US equities, where you expect a 10% return and 15% risk. Now imagine that there is a potential market-moving event, such as an election. The election will either produce a very positive or a very negative year for the market. You assign a 50% probability to each outcome.

Under this scenario, you believe the market will produce an eye-watering 30% return if things go well. If the market-friendly candidate loses, results will be less good. Under this outcome you forecast that the market will fall 10%.

Using simple math the expected return for the market is still 10%. This is calculated taking the two expected returns, multiplying each by the respective probability of that outcome (50%) and then adding the result: (50%*30%) + (50%*-10%) = 10%. While you've forecasted fairly extreme outcomes, the net result is that the average of your two outcomes still suggests a 10% return to equities.

However, the standard deviation of expected returns is now much higher than in a typical year. While the math is slightly more complicated, using the simplified two scenarios outlined above the standard deviation of returns would work out to 20%, 5% higher than the typical 15% risk you might assign. Under this scenario, you would arguably own less US stocks.

The reduction in US equity ownership does not reflect a change in your return estimate, but rather a higher risk estimate. While this example is a bit extreme, it does illustrate that investors need to think in terms of both inputs – return *and* risk – as each has a distinct impact on the allocation.

Playing defense

Let's consider another example. An investor comes to believe that there is a heightened risk of a recession in the United States. Typically, the return to stocks is negative during a recession. Risk aversion pushes multiples down while a weaker economy hurts corporate earnings. The combined impact of lower earnings and lower multiples results in typically poor equity returns.

Rather than take a chance on stocks or high-yield bonds, investors will tend to embrace the modern equivalent of sticking money under the mattress, namely buying US Treasury bonds. An increasing premium on safety typically leads to strong bond returns.

If you came to believe that a recession was likely, the first change you would want to make would be to lower your expected return for US stocks. In order to keep things simple, let's say this is just a US recession and other markets are unaffected, something that is highly unlikely in the real world.

At the same time, if you expected a recession you would also want to change your return estimate for bonds. For starters, if stocks are under pressure it is also reasonable to assume high-yield bonds will be as well. On the opposite side of the risk spectrum, conservative assets generally perform well during a recession. Central banks lower rates to support demand. Lower rates in turn lead to better returns for bonds.

Given all of the above, a recession forecast would suggest several changes to your expected returns. You would likely want to lower your expected returns to stocks and high-yield and raise them for US Treasuries.

Rather than a 5.7% annual return for US stocks (see Chart 7.1), you now assume that US equities will lose 5% next year. You expect lower returns for high-yield bonds as well, at just 2%. As the Fed will be doing whatever it can to support the economy, interest rates are likely to drop and bond prices rise. So you raise your expected return to bonds to 3.50%. When you adjust these inputs, the portfolio naturally deviates from the long-term strategic portfolio (see Chart 7.8).

Chart 7.8: US recession portfolio at 9% risk

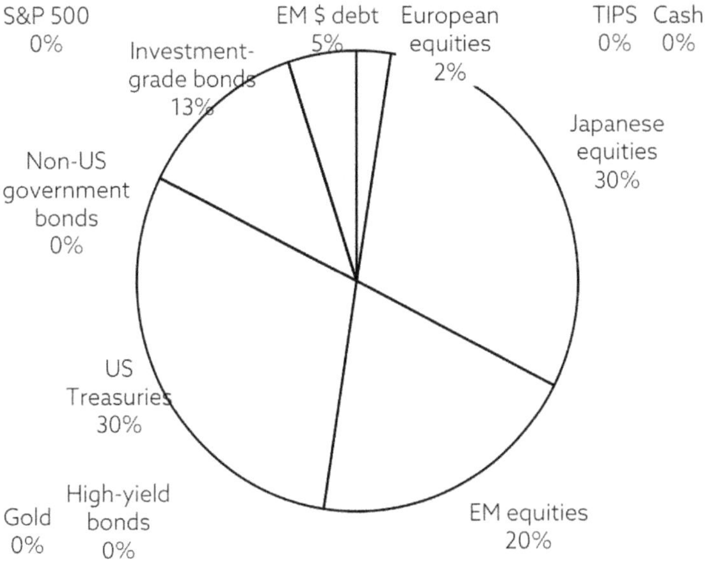

Source: Bloomberg, April 2017.

As you would expect, given the recession forecast, the resulting portfolio is more defensive than the previous one. The overall allocation to stocks drops from around 60% to close to 52%. All of the reduction comes from eliminating the allocation to US stocks. Why allocate to an asset class where you expect to lose money if there are other, more profitable options?

The focus on stocks in the United States reflects the fact that only the US assumptions changed. Had we also lowered the return estimates for other markets, the final allocation would look different. Again, this is not particularly realistic. It is highly unlikely that foreign markets would be unaffected by a US recession. But the simplicity of the change helps illustrate how the new portfolio deviates from the strategic portfolio.

While the optimization resulted in a slightly lower allocation to equities, it did not abandon the asset class entirely. Instead of the US, the allocation tilted towards Japanese and emerging market stocks. The process bought less of the asset class expected to produce negative returns and more of the asset classes expected to produce positive returns.

Beyond equities, the changes are actually more dramatic. The allocation to high-yield fell from 7% to 0%. The process effectively abandons high-yield. While the return reduction was modest, it still represented a fairly significant reduction in the overall return expectation for that asset class. Going from a 3.65% return, the original return forecast for high-yield (see Chart 7.1), to the more modest 2% return assumed in this scenario, cuts the return estimate by almost half. That will normally have a big impact on an asset's allocation.

Still, outside of high-yield the risk reduction was not as large as might have been expected. This leaves the question: why did a tactical shift predicated on a recession not have a more profound impact? After all, while the equity composition changed, the overall risk from equities remained broadly the same.

The reason is that while the above example assumes a change in return assumptions, the risk target remained the same. All the optimizer knows is that certain segments of the stock market and high-yield will produce lower returns. The concept of a recession has no practical impact on the portfolio.

The way to deal with this is two-fold. First, change all of the equity return assumptions, not just those for the United States. More importantly, lower the risk target. If there are concerns about a recession and equity market correction, take less risk.

While this iteration took insufficient note of the change in equity returns, the exercise was not a total bust. The model did respond to the underlying fear, a recession, in a different way.

The new portfolio has a dramatically higher allocation to government bonds. By raising the expected return of US Treasuries, even to a still modest 3.50%, the allocation jumped to 30% of the overall portfolio. This makes Treasury bonds, along with Japanese equities, the single largest allocation.

There are two reasons the allocation to Treasury bonds jumped so dramatically. First, government bonds, whether US Treasuries, UK Gilts or German Bunds, tend to be a low-risk asset class. The risk estimate for US Treasuries is slightly over 3%. For an investment with a low expected risk it does not take a particularly aggressive return estimate to spike the allocation.

Recall that a Sharpe Ratio of 0.50, particularly for one asset class, is more than respectable. To the extent this example assumes that US government bonds produce nearly a unit of return per unit of risk, the optimization will favor that asset class.

The second reason the optimization favored Treasuries is the covariance matrix. The covariance matrix is assigning a -0.36 correlation between US equities and stocks. As far as the process is concerned, bonds are likely to rise when stocks fall.

In a world in which stocks are more likely to go down, the process will favor any asset class with a negative correlation. This is also a good illustration of why investors should consider the source of volatility. Assuming the source of the correction is a recession, the negative correlation between stocks and bonds would probably hold.

However, if on the other hand the assumption is that stocks suffer because of an aggressive Fed, the investor might want to adjust the stock/bond correlation numbers. In that instance, bonds would probably not be an effective hedge against equity risk. One way to embody that view would be to change the period used to calculate the covariance matrix. For example, calculating the correlations based on a period such as early 2013, when US stocks and bonds sold-off in unison, would be one way to incorporate this view into the optimization process.

Finally, it is important to note that the covariance matrix also has a negative correlation between Treasuries and non-US equity markets. Based on this time frame, the historical correlation between Treasury bonds and Japanese equities was an even more negative -0.40. This suggests that Treasuries are even more effective in hedging non-US equity risk. This also helps explain the big jump in Treasury exposure.

Playing offense

The previous example embodies pessimism. What happens when expectations turn more exuberant? At the time of writing valuations are high, suggesting more muted expectations, particularly for US equities, are appropriate. That said, imagine an equity market sell-off that left valuations more reasonable. This next set of examples assumes a world in which more reasonable valuations suggest higher potential returns.

With that in mind, we make a number of changes to our stock market expected returns. All the non-equity return estimates revert back to the original estimates in Chart 7.1. However, the expected equity returns under this scenario assume better-than-normal returns, specifically for US stocks. The assumption is that non-US equity markets return 10%, with the US crushing all competition with a 20% expected return. In other words, this scenario reflects a US-led bull market. The resulting portfolio shown in Chart 7.9 reflects this US bias, but with some revealing twists.

The most obvious change is that the new portfolio has a 40% allocation to US equities. The allocation would have been even higher if not for a constraint: no more than a 40% allocation to any one asset class. That constraint represents a practical consideration that no single asset class should ever dominate the portfolio. Whether that constraint should be 25%, 40% or 50% is ultimately up to the investor and their willingness to allow for a more concentrated portfolio.

The spike in the allocation to US stocks comes at the expense of other markets. This raises the point, if we've increased the expected return not just for the US but also for other equity markets, why does the allocation to non-US Stocks drop?

Again, the reason goes back to the risk budget. The expected return to US stocks could be raised to 100%, but that doesn't change the fact that our risk budget is still only 9%. With a constrained risk budget there is only so much room for stocks in the portfolio. Add too much to equities and no combination of other asset classes will bring the risk down below 9%. This is also another reason to constrain the overall percentage of US equities. A portfolio with just US stocks is not diversified and will behave poorly if the return assumptions prove incorrect. All of which is just a geeky way of saying, "Don't put all your eggs in one basket."

Chart 7.9: Equity bull market portfolio

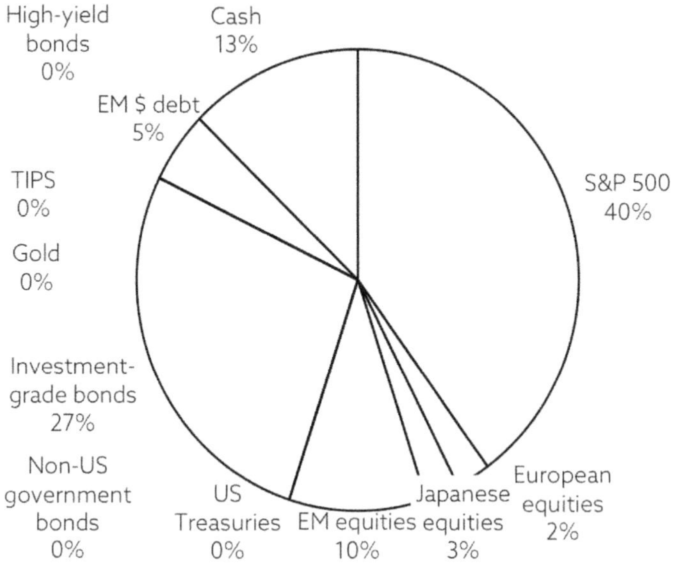

Source: Bloomberg, April 2017.

Given this constraint, the optimization will favor whatever asset class makes the best use of the specified risk budget. As in the previous example, the solution is to change the risk budget. While investors should not make a habit of shifting their risk budget, to the extent an investor has a strong view, either bullish or bearish, the only way to fully manifest that view is to be willing to change the risk target.

Outside of the equity allocation there are other important changes to the portfolio as well. As with the original strategic portfolio, there is once again a big weighting to investment-grade bonds. However, the allocation to high-yield fell out, despite the fact that the expected return did not change. With high-yield expected to return less than 4%, the allocation process heavily favored equities. With these aggressive return targets, why buy *equity-lite* bonds when you can own stocks producing double digit returns?

One final observation. The cost of the aggressive allocation to stocks is an increase in cash. Because cash has hardly any risk it is useful in dampening more volatile portfolios.

But what if an investor was uncomfortable with all that cash? After all, the dominant view is that US stocks will soar. It is not clear that an investor with such a bullish perspective would accept the opportunity cost of that much cash. For an investor that finds the resulting portfolio too conservative and inconsistent with their bullish outlook, the simple solution is, once again, to dial up the risk.

More than returns, risk is the most important dial at your disposal. Risk budgets should not be taken lightly, but nor are they carved in stone. They need to reflect investor circumstances and risk tolerance, but they can and should also reflect market views, at least to the extent the investor has particularly strong views.

Within the framework of portfolio construction, investors need to be *explicit* about their tolerance for risk. Rather than stumble into a riskier portfolio, an explicit risk target forces an investor into making a conscious choice. If you're particularly bullish, raise risk. When you're very concerned about financial markets, lower risk. This follows a basic tenet of portfolio management: try to be as clear and precise as possible.

Dialing up risk

For those willing, on occasion, to take the plunge and increase their risk budget, the contours of the portfolio will change dramatically. As an example, we can take the return estimates used to create Chart 7.9 but raise the risk target from 9% to 11%. The change results in a much more aggressive portfolio. We could call this the super bull portfolio (see Chart 7.10).

Chart 7.10: Equity super bull portfolio

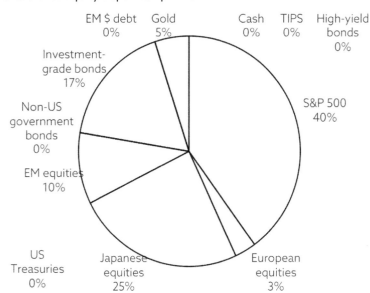

Source: Bloomberg, April 2017.

The obvious and intentional difference between the two portfolios is that the latter is riskier. Almost all of the incremental risk comes from increasing the equity allocation. The super bull portfolio has a 78% allocation to global stocks versus a little under 63% for the 9% risk portfolio. For those used to thinking in terms of allocations, the resulting portfolio is much closer to a traditional 80/20 stock/bond portfolio.

The majority of the incremental equity exposure comes from Japanese stocks. Why Japan? As with the previous example, the optimization was run with a constraint that prevented the process from loading up exclusively on US equities.

While some might question the constraint – why not buy more of the asset class you're most bullish on – this is a sensible precaution. These are after all *forecasted* returns. The forecasts may be wrong and the investor wants a portfolio that helps protect her from herself. While constraints should be used judiciously, it is reasonable to avoid a portfolio that is effectively a one-way bet on a single asset class.

With a bigger risk budget and the US equity allocation constrained, the optimization process becomes an exercise in finding the next best alternative. This is why the process added exposure to Japan. Japan has a lower risk estimate, consistent with historical patterns, than emerging markets. Based on these assumptions the Japanese equity market offers better risk-adjusted returns than simply buying more EM companies.

This still leaves Europe. By design Japanese and European equities have the same return assumption, 10%. They also have similar risk estimates, about 17% each. Why then does the process favor Japan over Europe?

During the period over which the covariance matrix was estimated, Japan had a modestly lower correlation with US stocks than Europe. As US stocks represent the biggest bet in the portfolio, the process will tend to favor the equity market with a lower correlation to the United States.

Should an investor be uncomfortable with the allocation, they have a few choices. One would be to add a second constraint limiting the allocation to Japanese equities. Another could be to raise the expected return for European or emerging market stocks. A third option would be to adjust the risk or correlation assumptions for Japan.

Dials to turn

This process illustrates another benefit of the optimization. If the investor is uncomfortable with the result of the optimization, there are multiple levers that can be used to make adjustments. Playing with the results and thinking about the underlying assumptions will force a series of decisions. Are the return estimates in the range of what is desired? Is the historical period selected to estimate correlations indicative of what is expected going forward? Is the risk estimate for a given asset class too high or too low?

While the allocation produced by the optimizer may not be what was expected, it may nevertheless be a more efficient portfolio than the one that was originally envisioned.

Impact of risk on allocation

In all of the previous examples, the focus was on tactical changes to return assumptions. This is consistent with the way most investors think. Much more time is spent thinking about return rather than risk.

However, as discussed previously, returns are harder to forecast than risk. Consider the example of the financial crisis in 2008, when the S&P 500 lost more than a third of its value. Five years later it gained nearly a third. In the space of five years, a major asset class experienced a 70 percentage point swing in annual returns. Obviously, the riskiness of stocks also changed during this period. The difference is that the magnitude of the change in risk was smaller than the magnitude of change in returns. Put more simply, returns tend to move around more than risk.

That said, there are instances when risk spikes, occasionally by quite a lot. Should an investor have a view on risk, they should also incorporate that view into their tactical asset allocation.

A recent example comes from Chinese equities. Chinese stocks are volatile, even under normal conditions. The equity market in China is still in a relatively early stage of development. The onshore A-Share market tends to be dominated by retail investors who are often far more interested in chasing winners than the fundamentals of a company.

One archetypal story is of a Chinese cement company. During the boom years of late 2014 and early 2015, cloud computing companies were the market darlings. In order to take advantage of this trend, the cement company changed its name to Cloud Cement. Investors dutifully responded by doubling the market value of the company the next day.

From the summer of 2014 to the summer of 2015 the on-shore market in Chinese stocks surged as investors chased winners. During this period not only was the market rising at a stupendous pace, but it was doing so in a remarkably straight line. With the exception of a brief pullback in early 2015, and later that spring, the ascent was characterized by a steady grind higher. Until of course the trend went into reverse.

Starting in mid-June of 2015 the Chinese market began to sputter. With the exception of an aborted rally in late 2015 the market did not bottom until early 2016. At one point near the lows, a measure of short-term volatility on Chinese equities hit around 70%.

A market that had been a stellar and reliable performer for a year abruptly turned into a risky and money-losing proposition. Investors panicked as officials adopted several ill-fated regulatory changes, most of which backfired, to stem the bleeding. In this type of environment, not only did returns plunge but volatility surged.

And what happens at the country level can occasionally occur to an entire asset class. Consider the recent example of emerging market stocks. Emerging market equities peaked in the spring of 2011. Following a short bear market these stocks spent the next four years in a trading range, gaining little ground while stocks in the United States and other developed markets enjoyed a strong bull market.

Chart 7.11: MSCI Emerging Market Index 90-day volatility (%)

Source: Bloomberg, April 2017.

However, beginning with the bursting of the Chinese equity bubble, emerging market equities experienced another sell-off. The broad MSCI Emerging Market Index fell by 35%. During this bear market the 90-day volatility of the MSCI Emerging Market Index rose from 11% in June of 2015 to over 20% later that fall (see Chart 7.11).

Then a funny thing happened. Valuations got low enough to entice buyers and the outlook for the global economy improved. After being out of favor for years, investors rediscovered the asset class.

As EM stocks started to rally the volatility of the asset class fell by nearly 50%, from 21% in late 2015 down to 9% by the spring of 2017. In the space of approximately 15 months the risk of this asset class fell by more than half.

For an investor thinking about an allocation to EM equities this type of shift in volatility has a profound impact. Depending on the time frame used to estimate risk, an investor would get wildly different estimates of volatility for emerging market stocks. In turn, these different risk estimates would lead to very different allocations.

One solution, similar to how to deal with volatile return estimates, is just to select a long horizon to estimate risk. An industry standard is around 60 months of data. The theory is that a longer period will smooth out the good and bad times and produce a more stable estimate of risk. The problem is, as the above example illustrates, in the short term risk can deviate significantly from that long-term average. In some circumstances it is worth considering adjustments to risk estimates.

Let's return to the initial example from earlier in this chapter. Consider what happens when you leave the return assumptions untouched but change the estimates of risk. The original risk estimate for EM equities was 21%, reflecting the heightened volatility of the period, June 2014 through July 2016, used to estimate the covariance matrix (see Chart 7.1).

Let's say a forward-looking investor believes that emerging market countries have permanently stabilized. The thesis assumes that EM countries are now on sounder footing. Given less volatile fundamentals, the investor assumes that future volatility will be closer to the more recent period of spring 2017, with risk at around 10%.

Using the original return estimates, a 21% EM risk estimate and a 9% portfolio risk target, the allocation to EM equities was around 10%. If you then change the volatility assumption to 10%, the allocation to EM triples, from 10% to 30%. EM equities are now the largest holding in the portfolio, even larger than US equities (see Chart 7.12). The only reason it was not even larger was that the optimization was again constrained for a maximum to any one asset class. After all, few investors would sleep well holding half their allocation in EM stocks.

Chart 7.12: Emerging market low-risk portfolio

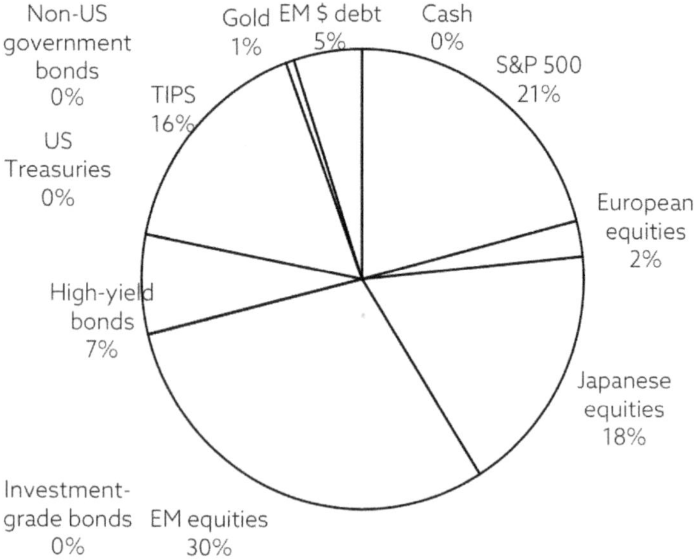

Source: Bloomberg, April 2017.

The key point here is that the sharp rise in the EM allocation occurs with no change in the return estimate. Instead, what changed was the denominator in the EM Sharpe Ratio. In the first set of assumptions it was assumed that the asset class would generate around a 7% return. The return was competitive with the other asset classes, but bought at the price of more than 20% annualized risk. With the risk estimate cut in half the Sharpe Ratio doubles. In a risk-controlled portfolio this dramatically increases the appeal of the asset class.

The EM example illustrates one of the most important conclusions of this chapter: when doing asset allocation, think in ratios. Return without risk lacks context. Add correlation to the mix and you have all the inputs you need to build any portfolio.

Key concepts: tactical portfolio shifts

➤ Tactical views will tilt a portfolio away from the long-term, strategic allocation.

➤ Consider changes to both risk and return assumptions when making tactical adjustments.

➤ Another tool to consider is changing the risk budget, raising it when expecting particularly high returns and lowering it when concerned about a bear market.

Conclusion

A T THIS POINT I expect some readers may be a bit disappointed. Nowhere has the book provided guidance on making a killing in the stock market, or how to trade commodities. On the other hand, hopefully it is clear by now that was never the intent.

For those still looking to get rich quick, it may be some consolation that a well-developed asset allocation strategy does not prevent aggressive investing. Nor does it prevent excessive conservatism. The goal is up to the individual investor or their advisor. The point of asset allocation is to find the most direct route towards that goal.

This book started with objectives and constraints as they, not a market forecast, ultimately drive what the portfolio should look like. The process of building a portfolio starts once the investor's goals are set and limits defined.

That is when the real work of asset allocation begins. Once the investor knows what they want (objective), what they can do (skill) and what they are willing to do (constraints), they can begin to build a portfolio. Hopefully if nothing else this approach makes portfolio construction, if not simple, at least more methodical.

Keep it simple

In an effort to make asset allocation simpler, much has been left out. For the most part, this was intentional. As some will have noticed, the book did not spend much time talking about less traditional asset classes, such as hedge funds. Nor did the book attempt to settle the debate of whether investors should rely on active or passive funds.

It is not that these are not important topics, but investors can build successful portfolios either way. Yes, hedge funds can be additive to a portfolio if they can produce a differentiated, uncorrelated return. That said, most investors will do well to first focus on getting the basic ingredients in the right mix. Those who are looking to add hedge funds and more esoteric asset classes probably have little need for this book in the first place.

Similarly, the debate between whether to use active or passive funds is not crucial to the asset allocation process. Suffice to say for most investors the answer is probably to use a mixture of both. A few active funds, where it is believed that the manager can add value, coupled with ETFs, are more than sufficient ingredients to build a robust portfolio.

While asset allocation will never be simple, it can be made simpler. The key is having a framework. This breaks the process into a series of more manageable steps and also provides a few key principles to guide the process.

Why it's worth the bother

Hopefully the book has provided that framework in the form of a governing philosophy as well as a series of steps that define the process. While every investor will not follow every step – most won't try to construct their own asset class return models – there is a benefit to knowing the process, even if it is not always followed.

Before summarizing the key steps and principles, it is worth reiterating why all of this matters in the first place. As stated repeatedly, the goal of asset allocation is not to get rich, at least not quickly. Nor will asset allocation, no matter how faithfully followed, magically transform a bear market into a 10% return.

If anything, sometimes a sensible allocation will leave money on the table. Had anyone followed the advice in this book religiously they would have missed out on some of the spectacular gains in technology stocks in the late 1990s, or the phenomenal gains to be had in housing and banks stocks last decade. So why bother?

Because even though asset allocation won't make you rich quickly, it will let you accumulate wealth consistently. Asset allocation is not alchemy, but a better designed, more robust portfolio is likely to improve returns over the long term. A small annual increase in returns may not seem worth the trouble, but over a multi-decade period even a 1% increase in annual returns will make an enormous difference to an investor's wealth.

Chart C1: $50,000 retirement account compounding

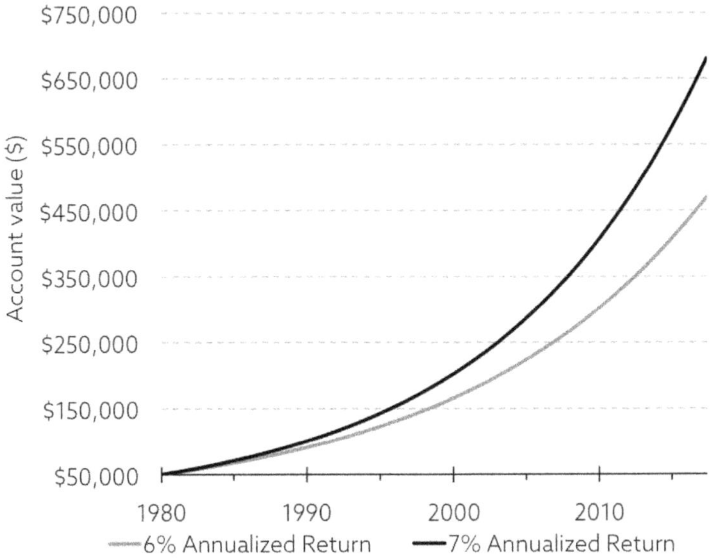

Chart C1 shows that for a theoretical investor starting out in 1980, the difference between a 6% and 7% return translates into an extra $210,000 at retirement. For those whose goal is to retire sooner rather than accumulate a bigger nest egg, the difference is equally profound.

Imagine a theoretical couple that decided they would retire when their savings hit $500,000. The couple that was able to produce a 7% annualized return would have been able to retire 5½ years earlier. That represents roughly 2,000 extra days to enjoy retirement. That is one, very tangible benefit to a well-designed portfolio. Asset allocation can help to create just that. Note that in this example I have ignored taxes. Governments would arguably not be as generous as this, but you get the point.

Protecting investors from themselves

There is a second, even better reason to focus on asset allocation: a portfolio better aligned with an investor's risk tolerance is more likely to keep them invested. As numerous studies have demonstrated, the biggest obstacle for most investors is themselves.

Human brains are not hardwired for investing. Our natural instincts often cause us to sell and buy at exactly the wrong times. From a financial perspective this means that too many investors can't or won't stick to an investment plan. Indeed the biggest challenge for most investors is not too much risk but too little commitment. This is an enormous challenge. No portfolio, no matter how much love and attention the investor lavishes on it, will work if the investor cannot stay invested for the long term.

To the extent that an investor can build a well-diversified portfolio that is aligned with their risk tolerance, there is a better chance they'll stick with their long-term strategy. In this sense, portfolio construction and risk management serves the same purpose as Odysseus having his men tie him to the mast of his ship in order to hear the sirens: it helps lessen the temptation to do something really stupid.

Five rules and a checklist

While the goal of asset allocation is straightforward, the methods can be confusing. There are a lot of moving parts. As you get to the more difficult parts, notably forecasting returns, there is no single recognized method. At this point, no matter what the experts tell you, the process is as much art as it is science. Nobody has yet perfected a foolproof way to make better-than-market returns. Investing requires risk. The key is how to manage and control that risk.

In that spirit, even if you ignore part of what has been recommended here, it is still useful to at least adopt a few key rules and steps to guide the process. These apply regardless of the exact method that is used to forecast returns or quantify risk. In that spirit, what follows are *five rules* and a simple checklist to guide the process.

Five rules to follow

1. Start with a goal

When building portfolios the investor needs to be clear about the objective. Get in the practice of translating qualitative life goals, i.e. the investor wants to retire in 30 years, into financial metrics, such as total return or income. Remember, the portfolio will be more influenced by goals and risk tolerance than by opinions about stocks or bonds.

2. Be both explicit and parsimonious when it comes to constraints

Constraints in portfolio construction are no different than constraints in any other activity. They limit, hopefully in a helpful way. When building a portfolio, the investor should be explicit as to what they're unwilling to do, whether this involves an asset class, geography or investment style. However, they should be wary of too many or irrational constraints. Constraints will limit the opportunity set and lead to less efficient portfolios.

For this reason it is often worth going through the exercise of building a portfolio with and without constraints (using a formal optimization process will help with this). This allows the investor to see the potential impact of constraints and whether they should reconsider if they really want these constraints.

3. Be honest about risk

Risk is the biggest and most important constraint. As such it deserves special consideration. Investors need to be honest with themselves about how much risk they can bear and how much money they're willing to lose. There are many ways to get to this point. Wealth managers often use questionnaires. Some are now turning to social media tools. Unfortunately, none of these methods are foolproof. Knowing when an investor is likely to abandon an investment strategy because they can no longer take the pain is critical. This is where most people fail. Not because their investment views or plan were bad but simply because they couldn't follow them. It is better to know the investor's limits up front and incorporate them directly into the plan.

4. Diversify

More return equals more risk. If investing ever seems too easy, you're probably about to lose money. Generally, making a lot requires being willing to lose a lot. Diversification is the only, partial exception to this rule. Diversification will not prevent a loss on any one investment. It will, however, over a very long time horizon, help avoid losing money on all assets at once. Diversification will sometimes require investing in places and assets that are less comfortable. The investor should take the time to get comfortable. A narrowly structured portfolio and a reluctance to venture outside of the investor's home country is not a winning formula.

5. Remember the denominator: always think in terms of risk-adjusted returns

To build an efficient portfolio some math is needed. Fortunately, it is less than most people think. You can still enjoy a well-tuned car without fully understanding all the workings of an internal combustion engine. However, as with a fast sports car, there are a few concepts the investor needs to be familiar with to avoid crashing the portfolio. In finance the most important concept is to think in risk-adjusted terms. While imperfect, the standard deviation of returns is a practical, short-hand way to measure risk.

The checklist

Many industries, from healthcare to airlines, have adopted checklists. Airlines realized long ago that a specific checklist helps reduce pilot error. Numerous studies have confirmed the same approach for surgeons. While portfolio mistakes rarely lead to immediate loss of life, the concept is equally valid. Building a portfolio may not be brain surgery, but it is difficult enough. It helps to reduce the process to a step-by-step approach.

1. Set a formal risk budget

This is by far the most abstract step, but arguably the most important. Trying to build a portfolio without a risk target is akin to driving a car without any knowledge or concern about how fast you're going. If things work out you'll get to your destination faster. If they don't, you crash. While a risk budget won't prevent a crash it will ensure that the investor is driving within their comfort zone. If the idea feels too abstract for a given client, you could match their risk budget to a stock/bond allocation that seems the most comfortable for them.

2. Define the opportunity set

Once the investor has a risk budget, the next step is developing a sense of where to spend it. Before putting money to work, the investor should be explicit as to what and where they'll invest. While some investors enjoy picking stocks or buying real estate, at a basic level a solid, long-term portfolio can be built with a relatively small list of mutual funds and ETFs. For those who believe they can add value with individual securities, i.e. picking individual stocks or bonds, these can also be added to the list of potential investments.

3. Check that the list of potential assets is diversifying

Avoid fishing in just one pond. If an investor is only willing to invest in companies domiciled in their own state and local real estate – some people actually do this – they're going to have a more limited, volatile portfolio than is necessary. Even conservative investors will benefit from some exposure to equities and asset classes that may be risky in isolation but provide a more diversified set of risk factors.

For those investors looking for maximum simplicity, this can be boiled down to a simple question: how did the various asset classes perform the last few times there was a bear market? If they all went down at the same time, consider adding asset classes such as gold, cash or government bonds that can help hedge a portfolio's downside risk.

4. Generate return and risk assumptions

These can be qualitative (high, average or low) or quantitative. Either way, follow a few general rules. First, make sure return estimates scale with risk, i.e. the riskiest ones should generally have higher return assumptions. Next, consider risk – both the level and co-movement of assets – when assigning weights. This is easiest to accomplish if a formal process is employed, such as a mean variance optimization, to construct the portfolio. MVO or another quantitative tool is the most effective way to build portfolios consistent with your risk budget and constraints.

5. Periodically monitor and rebalance the portfolio

Even if sticking to a strategic allocation, market movements will cause the portfolio to drift away from the target allocation. The portfolio will need to be periodically rebalanced in order to bring it back in line with targets. An annual rebalancing is a typical time frame. For those incorporating more tactical views, a quarterly review and rebalancing is a reasonable compromise between maintaining a long-term focus and adjusting for new information.

Asset allocation in five lines

The above is not intended as an exhaustive list. Instead, think of this as the stripped down asset allocation approach. Skilled investors can probably do better by adjusting their allocation based on a host of factors. Investors convinced that they can pick securities, or who can reliably find professionals to do it for them, can add return through security selection rather than relying just on market returns. Investors with access to more esoteric asset classes, such as hedge funds or private equities, may be able to further enhance their returns over the long term.

But whether you're building a portfolio for yourself or a client the basic rules still apply. And if the above checklist and principles still seem like too much, here is one final, minimalist summation. A poem for asset allocation.

Specify goals
Few but explicit constraints
Diversify
Modest return assumptions
Always, always adjust for risk

Index

Note: Page references in **bold** refer to charts